THE NATIONAL INTERESTS
OF THE UNITED STATES

IN FOREIGN POLICY

SEVEN DISCUSSIONS AT THE WILSON CENTER

DECEMBER 1980   FEBRUARY 1981

EDITED BY PROSSER GIFFORD

WOODROW WILSON INTERNATIONAL CENTER FOR SCHOLARS

University Press of America

Copyright 1981 by the Woodrow Wilson International Center for Scholars

Co-published by University Press of America POB 19101 Washington DC 20036

ISBN (Perfect): 0-8191-1787-0
ISBN (Cloth): 0-8191-1786-2

Each author was asked to address the questions as an individual
and not as an official. The views expressed are not to be understood
as institutional declarations of policy by any of the participants.

In order to facilitate readibility, footnotes have been eliminated
except in cases of direct quotation or citation.

WOODROW WILSON INTERNATIONAL CENTER FOR SCHOLARS

Smithsonian Institution Building

Washington, DC 20560

TABLE OF CONTENTS

INTRODUCTION

In November 1980 the senior staff of The Wilson Center judged the time ripe for some fresh thinking about the national interests of the United States. How could we stimulate it? We decided to ask two regional experts to speak to the national interests of the United States in each of six major regions of the world: the Soviet Union, East Asia, Latin America, Africa, the Middle East, and Western Europe.

To ensure that there would be some comparability among the assessments made for different regions, we drew up a list of questions to put to each of our principal speakers:

1. What do you assume to be the national interest of the United States with respect to [the region]?

2. What are the most important likely developments in [the region] during the 1980s?

3. To what extent can or should the United States seek either to accommodate, or alternatively to modify, these prevailing regional dynamics?

4. Is the pursuit of U.S. aims in [the region] likely (a) to complicate relationships with other regions; (b) to have important domestic costs and benefits in the United States?

Having identified scholars or practitioners who knew the region in question, who could write clearly, and who had some experience with the real constraints on policy, we asked them to answer these questions in 15 double-spaced pages.

We began our evening discussions with one on the Soviet Union on December 4th, because the relationship between the United States and the Soviet Union is the reference point for many arguments over strategic arms, arms control, world order or disorder, the linkage between security and economic policies, and differences among America's allies.

The discussion of East Asia on December 15th led immediately to a consensus on the importance of the U.S. domestic economy. Without a strong economy at home, the United States is a less dependable ally, is less confident about its partnership with Japan, and may be more apprehensive about the growing economic power of the newly industrializing entities of the Pacific perimeter (e.g., Korea, Hong Kong, Taiwan, Singapore, Australia). A United States inclined toward protectionism is not likely to act to sustain an open world trading system, even though that system coincides with its long-term interests and permits new emergent economies (Nigeria, Brazil) to enter significantly into world trade. Our speakers emphasized the positive economic and strategic benefits that could accrue to the United States from active participation in the evolution of a Pacific Basin community.

There was disagreement that evening about the degree and nature of "burden sharing" in defense that the United States should urge upon Japan, about whether West Europeans should be encouraged to sell sophisticated arms to China (there was agreement that the United States should not), and about the degree of alarm with which the United States should view the apparent recent alignment of India with the Soviet Union.

The next three sessions were devoted to Latin America, Africa, and the Middle East. They all raised questions about the priority the United States should give to countering Soviet-Cuban efforts at "destabilization" or "revolution" in, for example, Central America, Angola, and Ethiopia. Are these Soviet involvements critical to U.S. interests? or merely marginal opportunities for the Soviets arising from existing inequities, deeply divided local leadership, and thwarted development? While it is clearly desirable that the United States support centrist regimes and transitions to democracy from authoritarian rule (of the kind that have occurred in Spain, Portugal, and Peru), how adequate can such policies be unless they are conjoined with significant development funds, continued pressure for basic human rights, and concern for the long-term economic well-being of national populations rather than elites?

Significant disagreement was evident during these discussions on the following issues: (a) How dangerous for the whole of Central America is the smoldering civil war between left and right totalitarianisms in El Salvador? (b) How high a priority should be given to the debt problems of Brazil and the need they suggest for restructuring the flow of reinvestment of petro-currencies? (c) Since the United States wishes to maintain access at market rates to the strategic minerals of Southern Africa, can it deal with South Africa in ways that do not alienate its black population and the "frontline" states? (d) Is not acceptance of a Palestinian state a necessary precondition for further progress toward stabilization in the Middle East?

The Middle East discussion led inexorably to Europe: European (and Japanese) dependence upon Middle Eastern oil is far greater than that of the United States, and thus should result in European contributions to supply-line defense and Persian Gulf stability. In return, however, Europeans would expect greater consultation on other Middle East issues, including the nature and future of the Palestinian cause. These points were made forcefully by speakers in the European dialogue, as part of a general insistence upon the crucial importance to the United States of sound working relationships with its allies. Strategic and conventional force planning, the maintenance of an open world trading system, the increase -- or at least stability -- of world energy supplies, effective constraint of Soviet "adventurism," and positive changes in the prospects for Third World democracy -- all require careful and consistent action with allies. To expect, for example, that West Europeans would set conditions upon certain kinds of Soviet behavior is illusory unless the United States is willing to discuss a wide range of issues where American and European interests pull in potentially differing (though not opposed) directions.

What is true for Western Europe is also true for the Pacific: The United States needs to use to better effect the institutions that exist for regular consultation. Concerning some global issues, Japan has necessarily to be involved with West European nations directly rather than through American mediation.

Following the six meetings addressed to major regions, The Wilson Center held in early February a final meeting to synthesize and to put in order of priority the conclusions from its earlier discussions. Three papers from that final session are included in this volume: the reflections of James Billington about the non-material aspects of national interest, a summary of the observations of our three principal speakers on that occasion, and a concluding essay by Donald Nuechterlein, a participant in all the meetings from outside the Center, who brought to the whole venture an independent point of view.

The two papers presented at each of the six meetings are followed by a summary of discussion at that meeting. We have not attempted to erase the stylistic differences among papers or among the summaries prepared by different rapporteurs. We have permitted authors to speak in their chosen tones of voice. Unsigned commentary is that of the editor.

In addition to thanking our authors, who responded on short notice, we wish to convey our appreciation for the work of many of the staff at The Wilson Center who cheerfully participated in sharing the secretarial, organizational, and editorial tasks of this series. We also express our appreciation to Xerox Corporation, which through a special grant made the series financially possible.

Prosser Gifford

CONTRIBUTORS

JAMES H. BILLINGTON is director of The Wilson Center. A former professor of history at Princeton, he is a Soviet specialist and the author of The Icon and the Axe and Fire in the Minds of Men: The Origins of the Revolutionary Faith.

ROBERT R. BOWIE is Clarence Dillon Professor of International Affairs, Emeritus, at Harvard. He has taught law at Harvard, has held a number of positions in the U.S. government, most recently as the deputy director for national intelligence in the Central Intelligence Agency, and is the author of Shaping the Future and Suez 1956.

ALEXANDER DALLIN, formerly director of the Russian Institute at Columbia and a Wilson Center fellow, is professor of history and political science at Stanford. His works include German Rule in Russia, 1941-1945 and The Soviet Union at the United Nations.

THOMAS O. ENDERS, a career Foreign Service officer, has served in Stockholm, Belgrade, Phnom Penh and as assistant secretary of state for economic and business affairs. He has been Ambassador to Canada and most recently was U.S. Ambassador to the European Communities in Brussels.

WILLIAM J. FOLTZ is professor of political science and chairman of the Council on African Studies at Yale. He has written extensively on African domestic and international politics and is the author of From French West Africa to the Mali Federation.

PROSSER GIFFORD is deputy director of The Wilson Center. He has taught history at Yale and Amherst, where he was dean of the faculty. He has edited Britain and Germany in Africa and France and Britain in Africa.

LES JANKA, a consultant on the staff of DGA International in Washington, D.C., has been a senior staff member of the National Security Council. He was formerly assistant dean at Johns Hopkins' School of Advanced International Studies and has served as deputy assistant secretary of defense for Near Eastern, South Asian, and African affairs.

JAMES O. C. JONAH, a Sierra Leonean, is currently assistant secretary general for personnel services at the United Nations, which he joined in 1963. Among many assignments, Mr. Jonah has been political adviser to Gunnar Jarring, special representative of the secretary general to the Middle East, and to Lieutenant General Prem Chand, representative of the secretary general to Rhodesia.

ABRAHAM F. LOWENTHAL directs the Latin American Program at The Wilson Center. Formerly director of studies at the Council on Foreign Relations, his publications include The Dominican Intervention and Armies and Politics in Latin America.

RODERICK MacFARQUHAR is a Wilson Center fellow and copresenter of the current affairs program "24 Hours" for the BBC. A former Member of Parliament and editor of The China Quarterly, his works include Sino-American Relations, 1949-71 and The Origins of the Cultural Revolution, I: Contradictions Among the People, 1956-1957.

CONSTANTINE C. MENGES, a consultant with the Hudson Institute in Stanford, California and publisher of a monthly international political journal for the SAGE Association, is author of Spain: The Struggle for Democracy Today.

DONALD E. NUECHTERLEIN served in the Foreign Service and the Department of Defense. Currently a senior professor at the Office of Personnel Management's Federal Executive Institute, he writes on international relations and is author of U.S. National Interests in a Changing World and Thailand and the Struggle for Southeast Asia.

HUGH PATRICK is professor of Far Eastern economics and director of the Economic Growth Center at Yale. A specialist on Pacific economic development, he is coeditor of Mineral Resources in the Pacific Area: Papers and Proceedings of the Ninth Pacific Trade and Development Conference and editor of Japanese Industrialism and Its Social Consequences and of Asia's New Giant -- How the Japanese Economy Works.

ROBERT A. SCALAPINO is director of the Institute for East Asian Studies and Robson Research Professor of Government at the University of California, Berkeley. The editor of Asian Survey, his major books include Asia and the Major Powers, Communism in Korea, and Asia and the Road Ahead.

STEVEN L. SPIEGEL, a former research fellow at the Brookings Institution and Johns Hopkins' School of Advanced International Studies,
is currently associate professor at the University of California,
Los Angeles. He is the author of Dominance and Diversity: The International Hierarchy and The International Politics of Regions: A Comparative Approach.

ADAM B. ULAM is Gurney Professor of History and Political Science and
director of the Russian Research Center at Harvard. His works include
The Bolsheviks, The Rivals: America and Russia since World War II, and
Stalin: The Man and his Era.

JENONNE WALKER, most recently a member of the U.S. Department of State
Policy Planning Staff, is currently with the Foreign Service Institute.
She is a specialist on Western Europe and global human rights issues.
A former analyst of West European affairs with the Central Intelligence
Agency, she also served as executive assistant to then Director William
Colby.

DAVID WATT is director of the Royal Institute of International Affairs,
a visiting fellow at All Souls College, Oxford University, and a joint
editor of Political Quarterly.

LAURENCE WHITEHEAD, senior research scholar at The Wilson Center's
Latin American Program, is on leave from his position as fellow in
politics at Nuffield College, Oxford University. He recently edited
Inflation and Stabilization in Latin America.

SOVIET UNION

SOVIET-AMERICAN RELATIONS: WHERE DO WE GO FROM HERE?

Adam B. Ulam

What should and could be done about the Soviet Union's behavior in
the international arena has been the main preoccupation of American
foreign policy makers since 1945. Few would quarrel with the proposition that, starting already before the end of World War II, the main
thrust of Soviet foreign policies has been directed to expand the
power and influence of the U.S.S.R., and in a manner that has damaged
and threatened the national interests of the United States and its
allies. But what precisely has motivated the Kremlin in pursuing
this expansionist, and from our point of view dangerous and destabilizing course in international affairs? Here both Western experts
and statesmen have offered a variety of tentative explanations and
tried to fashion our own policies in accordance with the currently
most popular hypothesis. The average American might well feel that,
to paraphrase Marx's famous dictum, "The Kremlinologists have only
interpreted Soviet policies differently. The point is to change
them."

Whatever our analysis of the underlying motives and attitudes
that prompt the Soviet leadership on its present course, it is in
the highest interest of the United States to constrain and/or persuade the Kremlin to move in the direction of greater restraint in
its foreign policy. Today there is literally no area of the world,
no major problem confronting American foreign (and thereby much of
domestic) policy that can be considered apart from the activities
and attitudes of the rulers of the U.S.S.R. Our own national security, North-South relations, the energy problem -- none of these
can be isolated from what the Soviets are doing, and from what is
required to make them desist from those actions that, even when they
do not directly threaten the interests of the United States and its
allies, still contribute to and enhance the growing anarchy of
international life.

This trouble-making propensity of the Soviets' foreign policy
cannot be attributed solely or even mainly to the very nature of
their political system. The goal of making the whole world in
their own ideological image has not, since at least the late '20s,

been an important element in their political calculations and concerns. Indeed by the '50s it was tacitly recognized that Communist rule in a major power may become, as in the case of China, a source of danger rather than of comfort to the Soviet state. Yet by the same token the psychological residue of Marxism-Leninism, in conjunction with certain peculiarities of the Soviet political structure, has made it extremely difficult for the Kremlin to conceive of international life except in terms of rivalry and adversary relations among the superpowers. The Soviet doctrine of foreign policy appears to reverse neatly the old American maxim of considering other nations as "friends in peace, enemies in war." It was only in war and when fighting for survival, as between 1941 and 1943, that the U.S.S.R. could adhere to real alliance with other major powers. Once the most dangerous period of the war had passed, not to mention the peace that followed, the allies were viewed again either as rivals and hence potential enemies, or, in the case of smaller states, actual or future vassals. War, unless one promising an easy victory, has not been considered by the Kremlin as a viable option for achieving its foreign policy goals. At the same time its military superiority has been seen by Moscow as a vital ingredient of what it considers the most desirable configuration of international affairs: one where, without an appreciable risk of a major war, Soviet power and worldwide influence grow steadily, while those of the West are constantly on the wane.

What makes Soviet imperialism so difficult to live with is that, unlike that of major powers in the past, it is tied not only to what the rulers conceive to be the requirements of their national security, but also political security. No outside observer of the domestic scene in the U.S.S.R. can see even a remote chance of the Communist regime being overthrown or even seriously challenged in the foreseeable future. But the present leaders are what might be described as power hypochondriacs. A strike in Poland, relaxation of censorship in Czechoslovakia, a threat to the Communist rule in Afghanistan are seen by them not merely as normal vicissitudes of an imperialist policy, but as potential seeds of internal troubles in the U.S.S.R. Conversely, Soviet gains in Angola and Ethiopia on the one hand, and America's painful predicament in Iran and the travails of the West with OPEC, etc. on the other, are presented to the Soviet public as tangible proofs that for all of its vaunted freedoms and riches, the capitalist world has been doomed by the forces of history, while the Soviet system remains impregnable. Successful imperial expansion and the growing awe inspired abroad by Soviet military might provide reassurance to the rulers; and for their subjects these are intended to serve as advertisements of the regime's legitimacy and vitality.

It might be objected that the average Soviet man or woman in the street cares but little about the triumphs of his country's foreign policy and the consequent discomfiture of the West; his concerns are centered around the more mundane problems, such as frequent shortages of meat and other foodstuffs and the poor quality of other consumer goods. But one must not discount the real impact, be it at the subliminal level, of the appeal to national pride, nor discount that it may at least partially compensate the Soviet people for the deprivations they experience as citizens and consumers. "Soviet patriotism," i.e., Russian nationalism with an ideological varnish, is a potent force for social cohesion, all the more so now when the official doctrine has lost whatever persuasiveness and relevance it ever had for the majority of the Soviet people, and when mass terror is no longer employed to secure obedience and submission of the population.

A dynamic and expansionist foreign policy is thus built into the present rationale of the Communist regime in the U.S.S.R. Yet we would be mistaken to see it as an unalterable feature of Soviet politics. Should the risks and costs inherent in such a policy become so high as to threaten their domestic power base, the Soviet leaders would, as they occasionally have in the past, be prepared to change their foreign course in the direction of greater restraint and to seek at least a temporary accommodation with the West. As long as the Soviet system remains essentially what it is, it would be excessive to expect the rulers of the U.S.S.R. to adhere to the spirit of that rather excessively optimistic promise of the Nixon-Brezhnev declaration of 1972, in which to "avoid a dangerous exacerbation of their relations," both sides pledged not to seek "to obtain unilateral advantages at the expense of the other, directly or indirectly." But it is not too much to hope that, if confronted by a united, consistent, and purposeful stance of the West, the U.S.S.R. would seek to garner those sinful "unilateral advantages" through diplomacy, propaganda, and economic aid to the Third World, rather than by sending in soldiers, its own or Cuban, or by implicit threats posed by its rapid accumulation of strategic and conventional arms.

The story of what went wrong with detente offers an instructive lesson as to how closely Soviet policies are gauged to the Kremlin's perception of its protagonist's strengths and weaknesses. Mr. Brezhnev and his colleagues probably meant much of what they promised between 1970 and 1972, not because they had affixed their signatures on a number of documents, but because the general state of the world then urged prudence and caution on their part. The United States seemed to be on the point of disentangling itself from the Vietnam War and of shaking off the numbing effect it had had on both its domestic politics and foreign policy. The recent American opening toward China (or vice versa) threatened, were the Soviets to act incautiously, to become enlarged into an alliance or something close to it. With the United States emerging from its political malaise, Washington, unless propitiated by Moscow, might have concentrated its efforts on imparting a new momentum to Western unity, the impetus toward which had been stalled ever since the early '60s. There was also a real possibility the United States would accelerate the pace of the development of its new nuclear weapons systems.

But within little more than a year the Politburo's apprehensions of 1970-1972 had been revealed as excessive. Another domestic crisis superimposed upon the backwash of Vietnam went far in paralyzing the effectiveness of American foreign policy initiatives. Prospects for a closer integration of the West's policies once more proved ephemeral. How reasonable was it to expect the Soviets to adhere to the ground rules laid down by detente when, for all of its enormous economic, not to mention military, strength, the capitalist world proved incapable of parrying, or at least softening, the blow dealt to it by OPEC, most of whose members were entirely dependent on the West for military and industrial supplies, and ultimately for their national survival? Powers such as Abu Dhabi and Kuwait joined America's clients (e.g., Iran and Saudi Arabia) in inflicting this blow, more damaging in its ultimate implications to the interests of the United States and its allies than anything the Soviet Union has done since it became a superpower.

In 1976 a North Vietnamese general spelled out with admirable candor the reasons that convinced his government that it could with impunity break the Paris agreements of 1973 and move to seize the south: "The internal contradictions within the U.S. administration and among U.S. political parties had intensified. The Watergate scandal had seriously affected the entire United States...[It] faced economic recession, mounting inflation, serious unemployment, and an oil crisis."[1] One does not have to look for more complex explanations in order to understand why the Soviet Union decided that it could at little risk employ military power to promote its aims in Angola and the Horn of Africa, and why, if it did not instigate the Communist coup in Afghanistan in 1978, it then spread its protective mantle over it. The new threshold of Soviet imperial expansion was well and rather engagingly described by a Philippine fraternal delegate to the 25th Congress of the CPSU in 1976: "The confrontation of socialism with imperialism in Indochina has demonstrated that with the help of the Soviet Union one can achieve national liberation without threatening either world peace or detente." Because of Western sins of omission and commission (mostly the former), detente, rather than proving to be a restraining influence on the Kremlin's policies, has acted as a sort of sedative on those of the West. The Soviet Union has steadily escalated its use of force as an instrument of expansionist policies. With the new administration in Washington there were vague hints from Moscow that the Cuban contingent in Angola might be gradually withdrawn.[2] But then, evidently reassured by the confused and contradictory American stance on their use of surrogate forces in Africa, the Soviets continued to pursue and expand their Cuban gambit. Its more flagrant use in Ethiopia was then defended by Mr. Gromyko in

------

[1]New York Times, April 26, 1976.

[2]New York Times, May 26, 1977.

terms that seemed to imply the U.S.S.R. would at least refrain
from using its own troops outside what has been euphemistically
described as the "Socialist camp," and where presumably because of
the precedents of 1956 and 1968 the Soviets have the prescriptive
right to intervene whenever they choose. Said the Soviet foreign
minister, "Every fair-minded person should have a good word for
the Soviet Union, which has assisted a victim of aggression with
arms -- I repeat, with arms. Not one soldier with a rifle is in
Ethiopia."[3] But by December 1979 such delicacy and caution were
felt to be superfluous; presumably Soviet soldiers in Afghanistan
do carry rifles.

Mr. Carter's avowal that Soviet actions in Afghanistan had
taught him more about the U.S.S.R. than anything else he had learned
during his 3 -year stewardship of American foreign policy brings
to mind what a former secretary of state wrote: "Soviet military
moves which usually begin as tentative must be resisted early,
unequivocally, and in a fashion that gives Soviet leaders a justification for withdrawal."[4] An excellent piece of advice, but one
that the writer himself was unable to follow when the Soviets initiated their military moves in Angola, largely, to be fair, because
of congressional opposition to any strong countermeasures on our
side. Such measures, it was then widely believed in the United
States and Western Europe, might have jeopardized detente and
threatened a new cold war. It is not unreasonable to believe that
had the United States reacted to the Soviet-Cuban moves in Angola
with the kind of measures it was to adopt in the wake of the by then
far from tentative military intervention in Afghanistan, the whole
subsequent pattern of Soviet encroachments would not have taken
place. This paper is supposed to answer the question of what
extent our concentration on U.S.-Soviet relations might complicate
our problems in other regions, and what would be the domestic costs
of a more effective American policy toward the U.S.S.R. This question really ought to be turned around: Can the United States protect its vital interests in any area, and can it avoid really hor-
rendous domestic consequences if it cannot induce the Kremlin to
alter its present course in world affairs?

Much of the current thinking as to the ways and means of
achieving a modus vivendi between the two superpowers turns on two
assumptions. One sees the Soviet Union becoming increasingly en-
grossed in its domestic problems and troubles, and hence postulates
that eventually, hopefully soon, the very logic of its internal
development would force the Soviets to abate their international

---

[3]Pravda, June 3, 1978. With what diplomatic delicacy did Gromyko
acknowledge the presence then of Soviet officers who presumably
carry just sidearms!

[4]Henry Kissinger, The White House Years, New York, 1979, p. 569.

8

mischief making and seek a more cooperative relationship with this country. Hence what might be called born-again containment doctrine: we must be patient, avoid overreacting to Soviet moves, give an opportunity for new, more reasonable and prudent leaders in the Kremlin to prevail over their militantly inclined rivals.

The other formula echoes the almost equally venerable prescription of "negotiating from a position of strength." Our discomfitures and the Soviets' brazen behavior can be traced mainly to U.S. acquiescence to Russian military superiority, even and especially where strategic weapons are concerned. As long as this dangerous imbalance is not redressed in America's favor, the Soviets will continue to view us as being weak, and to conduct themselves accordingly. Some proponents of this explanation see the U.S.S.R. at some point quite ready to launch a preemptive strike against our missile sites. Others, though they do not take the Soviet marshals' apparent equanimity about nuclear war at its face value, still argue that without at least matching the Soviets' arms buildup, the United States must suffer continuous and ever more grievous setbacks to its prestige and influence, culminating in an eventual "Finlandization" of Western Europe, if not something worse.

Neither view, nor the doctrines from which they are descended, can be summarily dismissed. Yet whether taken separately, or even if somehow they could be combined, they do not add up to an entirely satisfactory prescription for obtaining a handle on our excruciating problem.

It is quite likely that during the coming decade the Soviet system will be subjected to considerable strains and stresses. Barring some biological miracle, the currently ruling oligarchy will almost simultaneously leave the scene -- a situation that even under the smoothest succession arrangements is bound to lead to a period of political instability and maneuverings for power at the top. And judging by the precedents of 1953-56 and 1964-65, the new leaders, until firmly ensconced in power, are very likely to seek a considerable lowering of international tension, and to speak the language of peace and cooperation. Some of the domestic issues that will require their attention are already clearly perceptible. There has been a notable slowing down of economic growth and productivity. Agriculture remains the Achilles heel of the Soviet economy. The differences in the birthrates of the various ethnic groups in the Soviet population will increasingly pose some uncomfortable dilemmas for the regime, which for all of its ideological trappings seeks and finds its main source of strength in Russian nationalism. Analogies with other Communist societies work very imperfectly in the case of the U.S.S.R., and nothing entitles us to anticipate developments similar to the "Prague spring" of 1968 and the "Polish summer" of 1980. But strikes and food riots have not been unknown in post-Stalin Russia, and they might well recur, and on a larger scale than those about which we possess information.

Problems concerning world communism are likely to become even more serious and perplexing to the Kremlin than they are at the moment. The present septuagenerian leaders have no reason to be unduly disturbed by the prospect of Communist China in the next 10-20 years becoming a major industrial and hence military power, but it is unlikely that their successors could afford such equanimity. The Brezhnev doctrine may soon be invoked to arrest or reverse the withering away of Communist power in Poland. Yet whatever happens there, no Soviet satrap in Eastern Europe will ever again feel entirely secure, and no Russian leader would disregard the probability of similar troubles erupting in other parts of his empire.

On the face of it, Mr. Brezhnev's and his colleagues' successors appear bound to inherit a lot of troubles that should keep them fully occupied and thus disinclined to keep adding to our own. Possibly so, but only on the assumption that the risks and costs they see as a consequence of continued misbehavior abroad become much higher than they have been during the last seven years, the period of what we still insist on calling detente.

Perhaps we should eschew terms like "detente" and "cold war," for in many ways they obscure, rather than clarify, the nature of relations between ourselves and the Soviets during the periods they are purported to describe. This comes out most vividly when we examine what has been called here the modified "negotiating from a position of strength" prescription for American policy vis-a-vis the U.S.S.R. Most of its proponents acknowledge that it would be virtually impossible, quite apart from any economic constraints, for the United States to surpass, perhaps even to match, the U.S.S.R. in every category of military strength in which the latter currently enjoys a quantitative advantage. Their main plea is therefore for strengthening the American strategic weapon arsenal to the point that would lead the U.S.S.R. to have no illusion that it could afford to launch a preemptive strike, or survive a nuclear confrontation. Yet when was it that the United States enjoyed the greatest margin of power over the Soviet Union? Undoubtedly between 1945 and 1955, not so much because of its first monopoly and then crushing superiority in nuclear weapons and their means of delivery, but because of its tremendous industrial strength while the economy of the U.S.S.R. was first in ruins, and then in the process of recovery.[5] Yet did America's strength stop the Soviets, in a flagrant violation of their wartime pledges, from taking over Eastern Europe, from blockading Berlin, and then unleashing the North Koreans on the south?

---

[5]The counterargument that the United States had demobilized between 1946 and 1950 and that the U.S.S.R. did not is not quite correct on the second count, and does not detract from the palpable fact that in view of America's crushing industrial superiority, amply demonstrated during the war, a "Soviet march to the Channel" had to be seen by Stalin as suicidal.

A powerful strategic force is indeed a necessary <u>precondition</u> of a successful foreign policy (and it was bad political psychology, even if technically justified, to let the Russians get ahead of us in certain categories of nuclear weapons), but by itself it could not persuade the Kremlin to reexamine and change the premises of their own policies.

We must then reexamine some premises of our attitude in world affairs. For example, the maxim "Speak softly, but carry a big stick" is quite inappropriate when dealing with the Soviets. We have indeed carried a very big stick, especially during the first 20 years after the war. But because, except for one occasion, we spoke too softly, this big stick did not prevent an erosion of American and Western influence, an erosion that in most cases did not come of itself, but was triggered by activities of the U.S.S.R. Nor do we have to envisage "speaking firmly" as being synonymous with political, not to mention nuclear, brinksmanship. Let us consider the combined economic strength of the United States, its allies, and Japan. Enormous though it is, it has never been translated effectively into political power. Western Europe between 1950 and the '70s presented a phenomenon, perhaps unique in history, of an area whose phenomenal economic growth has been paralleled by a steady decline in its worldwide influence. It is a dramatic reversal of this trend that is an absolute condition for a more satisfactory condition to West-East relations, and hence poses the most important challenge to American statesmanship.

Western unity and a powerful nuclear and conventional deterrent are not the only ingredients of a policy that could help usher in a happier era of peaceful coexistence between the two countries. The Soviets are not entirely unjustified when they complain that apart from anything else, it is the vacillating and inconsistent course of American policies that is the source of much trouble between the two countries. To be sure, granted the nature of our political system, we could not always adhere to what in the Kremlin's view should be a businesslike pattern of negotiations between the two superpowers. Had our policymakers understood what he was after, they still could not have endorsed Khrushchev's grand design, which, for all the threats and bluff in which it was veiled, was aimed to produce what Peking quite aptly characterized as "cohegemonism" of the two superpowers. But it is undeniable that the very style of our diplomacy has seldom been conducive to a realistic appraisal of the Soviets' hopes, fears, and real goals. Stern warnings to the Kremlin to mend its ways, usually with no clear idea of how to back them up, have alternated with illusory hopes and deceptive friendliness produced by the latest summit. An excessively legalistic and moralistic stance by Washington would be succeeded by, or sometimes incongruously combined with, over-eagerness to please. As I have written elsewhere, it is not only the obsessive secrecy in which Moscow's decision making is veiled, and camouflage thrown over its real hopes and fears, but also the excessive volatility of American foreign policy and the frequent diffusion of responsibility for its conduct that tend to undermine the mutual credibility that is a basic ingredient of successful intrastate relations and negotiations.

Can and should the United States seek to modify the Kremlin's domestic policies, and induce it to relax its grip on the nations within its sphere of influence? As has been implied throughout this paper, the very fact of the West overcoming its present disunity and vacillations is bound to have a beneficial effect on the Soviet domestic scene. Deprived of opportunities to achieve easy triumphs abroad, the Soviet leaders might well turn to internal reforms and liberalization as means of demonstrating the viability and vitality of their system. They might also conclude, some of them probably have reached this conclusion already, that their present methods of administering their empire have become not only anachronistic, but counterproductive, and that they should not stand in the way of the eventual "Finlandization" of East Europe.

It is, on the other hand, questionable whether such desirable goals can be achieved or substantially advanced by direct pressures emanating from the government of the United States. The Carter administration has erred by dubbing its on the whole admirable activities on behalf of human rights a policy. It is an obvious fact that our concept of what constitutes basic human rights (e.g., freedom from arbitrary arrest) is simply incompatible with the survival of the Soviet regime. It may appear as quibbling, but in view of the mentality of Russian rulers it is important that our appeals on behalf of victims of political and religious persecution in the U.S.S.R. be presented not in the guise of a governmental policy, but as a natural humanitarian reaction of a democratic society. It is through more effective foreign policies, i.e., through a convincing demonstration that freedom and power go together, that the West can best advance the cause of human rights in the U.S.S.R. and elsewhere. To end with another paraphrase of Marxian semantics, "The emancipation of the people of the Soviet Union must be the task of the people themselves."

SOVIET-AMERICAN RELATIONS IN THE 1980s:
WISHFUL THINKING ABOUT U.S. POLICY

Alexander Dallin

I

Soviet-American relations are here to stay. Un-American as it may
seem, we must realize that there are no instant solutions to Soviet-
American differences, that the Soviet Union is a global power,
active and ambitious, and that the United States will need to deal
with it, for better or for worse. What are our proper concerns in
this relationship?

Our economic interests in it are trivial. Our ideological
differences are not matters to be adjudicated by government action.
The legitimate zone of U.S. foreign policy concerns is Soviet
behavior abroad. The United States must aim at a stabilization of
the internnational environment and at a stabilization of the strategic relationship with the U.S.S.R. -- including a commitment to
the avoidance of nuclear war and an earnest effort at limiting (and
if possible, reducing) strategic arsenals. In a broader sense,
the United States needs to be prepared for the worst eventuality,
but must seek in every way to make the Soviet Union a responsible
and restrained actor in the international arena.

Several things follow from this approach: (1) The Soviet Union
is not about to collapse, nor are its people about to revolt. The
fewer illusions we have on this (or any other) score, the better.
(2) The Soviet Union has for the first time achieved global reach
as well as strategic parity with the United States. It cannot be
expected to behave like Liechtenstein or the Seychelles. It will
strive to maximize its role and influence wherever it can, a goal
not basically so different from the objectives of the other superpower, though its methods and style are likely to be quite different indeed. (3) Whether or not we like the Soviet system (and most
of us don't) is immaterial to the formulation of U.S. policy: foreign policy must not be a function of taste or morality. It must
not be the mission of the United States to change the internal
order of the Soviet Union or its economic system. Unless we adopt
a double standard, to pursue the goal of changing the domestic regime of another country not only violates international law but

13

invites a symmetrical counter-intervention in the United States.
Nor must it be the task of American policy to dismember the U.S.S.R.
into its ethnic component parts; such a counterproductive effort is
neither proper nor informed by a good understanding of attitudes
inside the Soviet Union. In any event, to advocate dealing with
the Soviet Union seriously and, where possible, cooperatively, does
not in any way presuppose a benign view of Soviet power or Soviet
intentions. (4) Soviet-American relations are no longer a "zero-
sum game" (if they ever were); it is essential for policymakers
at both ends to understand that agreements may benefit each side,
and that if an accord suits the perceived interests of one, it
does not mean that it is detrimental to the other's. (5) There
are many objectives the United States may seek to advance tacitly,
as by-products of our general policy orientation; they must be
neither explicit nor primary goals of American policy; in fact, to
make them such might be to frustrate their attainment. These include the promotion of human rights in the Soviet Union (including,
but not limited to, freer travel abroad and emigration for Soviet
citizens) -- a worthy goal that can best be advanced by quiet
diplomacy rather than by its use as a selective weapon hypocriti-
cally applied; helping give Soviet citizens an opportunity to get
to know the outside world better -- the underlying assumption here
is that (barring security matters) both we and the Soviet population have far more to gain than to lose from a multiplication of
interactions between our two countries; and finally, convincing
the Soviet elite that they have more to gain from getting along
with the United States than from confronting it.

        II

American relations with the Soviet Union have suffered from a variety of handicaps. The most enduring of these are of our own making:
they are conceptual. Over the years policymakers and advisers,
media and public opinion have erred both by naively dismissing evidence of Soviet behavior and purposes that clashed with wishful
thinking about a better world, and by naively assuming the worst
about an ostensibly undifferentiated and unalterable totalitarian
system committed to global conquest and revolution. Several propositions deserve to be better understood:

    (1) Soviet foreign policy does not follow a "master plan,"
a "blueprint," or a "timetable" as has at times been averred.
Studies have shown a changing mix resulting from an encounter of
prior images and assumptions by Soviet policymakers and advisers
with the real world, producing an imperfect learning process and a
half-hearted adaptation to the environment. Long-range visions and
"ideological" goals have often proved to be operationally irrelevant; Soviet decision makers have found the "classics of Marxism-
Leninism" decreasingly helpful in coping with a complex and often
confusing world. Instead they find themselves increasingly con-
sulting technical, scientific, military, or area specialists.

(2) Foreign policy architects have typically assumed that we are dealing, on the Soviet side, with a "unitary rational actor." If now and then someone has recognized the existence of divergences among Soviet spokesmen or publications, these have usually been dismissed as trivial, exceptional, or orchestrated to deceive the world. It is in fact essential to get a good sense for Soviet political life -- with its bargaining, deals and trade-offs, jockeying for influence and power, and efforts to maximize political resources and develop influential constituencies -- and for the range of issues in dispute, to be able to explain Soviet policy outcomes. More generally, the refusal of Western observers to recognize diversity of policy orientations and values within the Soviet elite, as well as the occurrence (and the prospect) of meaningful change in the Soviet system, constitutes a major blind spot in our understanding of Soviet affairs.

(3) One school of thought that has led to a dangerous caricature of Soviet reality explains Soviet behavior as essentially predetermined by the course of Russian history and the continuity of political culture, ostensibly characterized by peasant cunning and deception, total dependence on and service to the state, Byzantine posturing, as well as extremism rather than moderation. Leaving aside the dubious notion of national character, such an approach too often fails to acknowledge changes of values, attitudes, and political culture as state and society evolve, as well as the evidence of diversity both before and after the revolutions of 1917. To what extent traditional "Russian" features remain is a matter to be investigated empirically, not to be assumed or asserted in advance.

(4) Another school of thought that has distorted our understanding of Soviet behavior sees the U.S.S.R. as "communist ideology in power." Not only has international communism (as a single movement) irreversibly fallen apart (suffice it to think of China), but the various regimes controlled by Communists -- and even non-ruling Communist Parties -- have increasingly come to reflect values and objectives rooted in the particular national setting of a given country. The operational utility of Communist "ideology" is modest at best, as the practical problems facing the Soviet leaders can scarcely be dealt with by doctrinal stereotypes and quotation mongering. Communism may still play a residual role as a guide to the perception of the Soviet leaders, to the categories that structure their mind sets as a rationale for policies being pursued, and as one of several sources of ambition and activism that informs Soviet behavior. But again, the extent of the impact of "Communist" beliefs, variable as it is from case to case, requires investigation and specification rather than a priori affirmation. The point is not that Moscow would not like to see the world changed in its image; the critical question is what price the Soviet leadership is prepared to pay or what risks it is prepared to take for the sake of achieving these ends.

(5) Contrary to conventional wisdom, Soviet decision makers
have typically avoided taking (what to them appear to be) high risks
in pursuing agreed objectives. They have normally eschewed situations that are apt to lead to direct confrontations with other
strong powers, or else they have backed away from such "adventurist"
encounters (the Cuban Missile Crisis of 1962 and the U.S. nuclear
alert over the Middle Eastern crisis in October 1973 being two relevant examples). At the same time, as Soviet military and other
capabilities have dramatically increased in the 1970s, it is likely
that the threshold of what Soviet analysts deem an acceptable risk
has also risen.

(6) Not only does it make a significant difference -- to them
and to us -- just who is in charge in Moscow (consider, for instance,
the duel between Khrushchev and Molotov 25 years ago) but, no less
important, we must learn to act on the well-demonstrated proposition
that our behavior does affect Soviet conduct, controversies, and
calculus. Whether or not the Kremlin writes off the United States
as an unreliable partner; whether the Soviet leaders seek greater
economic and technological interaction with the developed world or
return to autarky; whether Soviet analysts understand the dynamics
of West German, British, or Chinese politics, or act on the basis
of ideological and bureaucratic stereotypes; whether Moscow perceives
the normalization of Sino-American relations as a normal and ultimately legitimate (if unpleasant) move or sees it as a prelude to
a military alliance in which the United States arms dangerous
extremists at the Soviet doorstep as part of a conspiracy against
the U.S.S.R. -- all this and much more depends in large measure on
how the United States and its friends behave, what they say, and
how Moscow perceives and interprets their purposes and policies.
It is fatuous to argue, as some self-styled political strategists
have, that the essence of the Soviet system is unchanging and that
therefore we need lose ourselves neither in details of Soviet politics and personnel changes, nor in agonizing surmises about the
illusory impact of our actions on the Soviet world view. In fact,
these critics contradict themselves when they then acknowledge that
Moscow responds to perceived U.S. weakness (e.g., in regard to Angola or Iran) by pursuing a more venturesome, forward policy.

(7) Neither space nor the technical nature of the argument
permits discussing at any length dominant assumptions about Soviet
military capabilities and doctrine. As careful studies have shown,
the assertion that the Soviet Union can win a nuclear war does not
appear to be the operational consensus of the Politburo. While
many Soviet military theorists do not subscribe to the American
concept of deterrence, the assumptions underlying the Soviet defensive buildup amount to the functional equivalent of deterrence --
plus war-fighting readiness if this should prove necessary. Obviously the Soviet Union would like to derive political benefits
from military power, but it has thus far been no more successful
than others (including the United States) in translating capabilities into tangible gains.

Finally, it must be recognized that -- along with a ritual belief in the "changing correlation of forces," which Moscow has claimed to be seeing for well over 60 years -- there has been genuine concern in official Soviet quarters about a new "encircle-ment" of the U.S.S.R. by a hostile coalition including the United States, China, Japan, and NATO Europe. The U.S.S.R. has also been worried about the looming American effort to regain military superiority. This is something, it is safe to say, that Moscow will not allow the United States to achieve, even if it takes a major arms race at a high cost to the Soviet consumer.

III

The 1980s promise to be years of exceptional fluidity. Recent efforts aimed at easing international tensions have largely back-fired. Economic crises and competition as well as new weapons technologies are likely to make for a serious destablilization of the international order. The SALT process is virtually at a stand-still. Additional nations may acquire nuclear devices. Insta-bility and failure in the Third World are again likely to create opportunities for great-power intervention. The Polish crisis suggests the possibility of a showdown in the Soviet backyard, prompting agonizing choices for both Moscow and Washington.

The prospects of instability are further heightened by the changes of leadership in Washington and Beijing, and the impending ones in Moscow. A turnover of the leadership generation in the Soviet Union cannot be far off. Regardless of orientation and competence, the next teams may well lack the previous commitment to a common search for solutions, the determination to avert nuclear devastation, and the willingness to operate with tacit understand-ings. Both the Soviet and the American governments will need to start from scratch; it is hardly an exaggeration to say that today neither has a coherent policy vis-a-vis the other.

There has been ample speculation about the likely direction in which the successor generation in Moscow will move. It is probably safe to say that it will be far more activist in domestic affairs, more willing and eager to abandon the "don't-rock-the-boat" attitude of the Brezhnev incumbency; but what its program will be remains guesswork only rarely buttressed by evidence. While there is apt to be pressure in the Soviet system for administrative and economic reforms, these need not have political ("liberalizing") counter-parts; nor need it follow (some optimists to the contrary) that such reformers would be more conciliatory on the international scene.

At least as compelling is the prospect of a more nationalist or even jingoistic Soviet Russian elite eager to "cash in" on the superpower status of the Soviet Union (which they, unlike their

elders, tend to take for granted). But their inclinations are apt
to be frustrated, if not confounded, by conflicting trends -- on
the one hand, pressures for consumerism, conservatism, and corruption in Soviet society; on the other, the objective reality of multi-
plying shortfalls and bottlenecks -- in economic growth rates, technological innovation, energy availability, industrial and military
manpower, managerial techniques, and other indicators that fore-
shadow an era of what one skilled observer has called "the politics
of stringency" in the years ahead.

Far from facing the future with confidence and with certainty
that it has the answers, the Soviet political elite is likely to
be rent by major bafflements and debates. Are experts, advanced
technology, and computers a tool of or a threat to the Soviet
establishment? Is the party becoming an increasingly irrational
redundancy or does it serve a functional task? Moscow seeks independent judgment yet fears spontaneity and dissent: it thus seeks
to square a political circle. Self-sufficiency versus international interdependence is the theme of another debate. So is the
question whether Moscow prefers stabilization or destabilization
abroad. The priority of welfare or economic development is perhaps
the central issue currently contested at home (development here
encompasses regional development, for instance, in Siberia). As
the Soviet Union faces shortages and stringencies, out of whose
hide must the cuts be taken as future budgets are drawn up?

The easy 1970s, when Brezhnev & Co. could be all things to
almost all Soviet men (and a few women), are over. Hard choices
lie ahead, and muddling through or marking time (as, for instance,
on energy policy) is not likely to do.

All this implies that future trends in the Soviet Union are
open-ended: not only because we do not know enough about them
(which is true), but also because as yet they themselves do not,
and cannot, know. As for the implications for Soviet foreign
policy, their thrust is ambiguous as well. Choices may be determined by variables beyond Soviet control, including perceived
threats and opportunities abroad. Among these variables, in all
likelihood, will be U.S. conduct and capabilities. It is precisely
this open-endedness that will require on the part of U.S. policymakers an uncommon degree of flexibility -- a trait not normally
available in superabundance.

IV

It goes without saying that the United States and its allies must
assure that gross strategic parity with the Soviet Union and its
allies is maintained. A good case can also be made for strengthening

the conventional military capability of the Western powers. But
the pursuit of a new superiority (even if sugarcoated as a "margin of safety") is (a) a chimera, (b) the invitation to a dangerous and expensive arms race, and (c) the deathknell of arms control;
mutually acknowledged parity is a precondition for arms limitation
agreements in which agreed constraints have symmetrical effects on
both parties. What is needed in fact, to deal with Moscow, is not
superiority but firmness, clarity, and consistency -- as well as an
understanding of what makes Moscow tick.

How best to steer Soviet leaders toward a more responsible
and restrained role in foreign affairs is a problem that exceeds
the bounds of this essay. Willingness to resort to both rewards
and penalties is an essential part of such a long-range political
strategy, which may well take a leaf from the field of behavior
modification.

One essential element that has often been lacking in U.S.
conduct is the ability to enunciate what would amount to a price
list of rewards and penalties -- and to stick to it (allowing for
quiet diplomacy). In this fashion Moscow could realistically
calculate whether it is or is not prepared to pay a given price
for a contemplated move -- whether in its judgment the trade-
off is worthwhile -- rather than later be surprised, confused,
and feel duped.

One implication of such an orientation is that, just as the
United States must respond to "undesirable" Soviet behavior with
negative measures (if only to deter adventurous and irresponsible
elements in Moscow from proceeding with impunity), so it must also
be flexible enough to provide positive recognition and reward for
Soviet moves that the United States can applaud. In this sense
"linkage" between different issue areas is entirely proper; the
United States must capitalize on those assets that Moscow lacks and
seeks (for instance, advanced technology). Where "linkage" is inappropriate is (a) tying U.S. policies to internal conditions in the
U.S.S.R., and (b) linking other policies and events to arms control
negotiations, in which presumably both sides should have an equal
interest in a successful outcome.

If the above is somewhat reminiscent of the outlook that
in the early 1970s inspired the attempt to deploy what Henry
Kissinger called a "web of interdependence," it must be made clear
that the calculus that undergirded detente was never fairly tested.
It is incorrect to argue that the events of recent years demonstrate
the failure of the concept; they do show the failure of the practice,
but the underlying notions were never given a chance; for one thing,
American politics has not allowed the pursuit of policies whose
payoff requires a time span extending beyond the next election;
for another, the policy was subverted by a series of measures and
interventions, from the Jackson-Vanik Amendment to the one-sided
way in which the "China card" was played.

Especially in the 1980s, American foreign policy makers will
need to be aware of the limits of American power -- indeed, the
limits of any "power." The age of American predominance is irreversibly gone. A fresh look at the record would also show a characteristic over-concentration on military means in dealing with
complex and recalcitrant problems around the globe. The United
States must also internalize the (obvious but often forgotten)
proposition that there are many problems abroad and many pressures
for social and political change that are not Soviet inspired and
not related to the East-West competition. A nearsighted and simplistic approach risks playing into Soviet hands by antagonizing
allies and neutrals alike. Washington will also do well to remember
that a loss of U.S. influence abroad need not mean a gain for the
Soviet Union; OPEC is only one recent example of the world community
moving away from the "tight bipolar model" that characterized the
years of the Cold War.

Nor of course must we revert to the primitive assumptions that
all communism is equally "evil" and therefore tar Chinese, Polish,
or "Eurocommunist" trends with the same brush as the U.S.S.R.;
that everything done in the name of anti-communism is good and in
our interest (as some of our would-be friends are sure to insist);
or that every "Marxist" or "Socialist" regime is a Soviet tool or
satellite. Such arguments reflect merely ignorance and political
naivete.

What was said earlier about Soviet politics also suggests an
earnest need for heightened American sensitivity to the way U.S.
actions are likely to be perceived and interpreted by various Soviet
publics, and to what uses they will be put in the political dialogue that will shape future Soviet policy.

V

An intelligent and sophisticated American policy toward the Soviet
Union faces a major obstacle in the form of U.S. domestic politics.
Primitive anti-Soviet feelings are so deeply embedded that any
politician, preacher, or demagogue can make hay by charging an
opponent with "softness" on communism. In American politics it
is always profitable to take a "tough" stand, never to show understanding of the other side. Yet the test of foreign policy should
be its effectiveness abroad, not grandstanding at home.

The task is further complicated by the considerable clout of
special interests and lobbies -- be they ethnic and racial groups or
defense industries -- and by the recent tendency of Congress to
deprive the executive branch of a free hand in the conduct of foreign affairs.

Politicans and journalists have contributed to a misperception of Soviet actions: the typical image of relentless Soviet advances and successes neglects the numerous and severe setbacks the Soviet Union has suffered and the further difficulties it is sure to face in the years ahead, from the vulnerability of its missile force to its virtual lack of any reliable friends abroad.

Finally, there is a characteristic temptation to play it safe by responding to ambiguous Soviet moves by indulging in "worst-case analysis." One problem is that this has an inherent propensity to convert an outside possibility into a self-fulfilling prophecy. Another is that in the process of acting on its conclusions we are likely to transform ourselves in the image of our adversary.

All this calls for a courageous approach to public education in international affairs. I will not pretend that we are likely to see it.

VI

In the past the United States has repeatedly missed opportunities to influence Soviet policy in a direction desired by the United States and has often misjudged Soviet intentions and motives. The record amounts to a textbook of costly lessons.

Perhaps the most general lesson to act on is to beware of leaving the making of policy toward the Soviet Union either to know-nothings or to know-it-alls. Instead, the answer must be first, to train, consult, and listen to experts who know something about the problems at stake; and second, to assure the multiple advocacy of alternative policies, so as to be certain that, in a world of bewildering complexity and imperfect information, different approaches and explanations have a serious hearing before crucial decisions are made.

All this will not ensure that things will go right. But unless it is done, they are sure to go grievously wrong.

DISCUSSION

U.S. NATIONAL INTERESTS IN THE SOVIET UNION

Adam B. Ulam presented a sophisticated version of what might be
described as a pre-detente consensus on Soviet-American relations.
Ulam believed that relations between the superpowers went considerably better during the 1960s when, despite a series of crises,
the Soviet Union sought a _modus vivendi_ with the United States,
which for its part attempted to synchronize its policies toward the
East with those of its European allies. During the 1970s, Ulam
argued, the Soviet and American leaderships variously failed to
communicate with each other, or they transmitted confusing signals; as a result, meaningful discussion of outstanding issues
became vastly more difficult. By the late 1960s, Ulam continued,
the possibility of a coordinated policy involving Western Europe
and the United States had evaporated as a result of the Vietnam
War, intra-European problems, political crisis in the United States,
and the emerging economic strains within the alliance. It is foolish to blame the Soviet Union for this state of affairs, Ulam
argued, for they were doing the sensible thing, in view of their
interests: seeking to take unilateral advantage of changes in
the international situation that favored them.

Western leaders and foreign affairs analysts, in attempting to
deal with these difficulties, have advanced a number of tentative
policies. What Ulam somewhat derisively called "born-again containment theory" counsels patience with the Soviet Union, an appreciation
of the problems faced by the Soviet leadership, and a disposition
to let the Soviets "suffer from indigestion by gobbling up too much
territory." According to Ulam, the crux of this position is a
belief in Soviet weakness and in the likelihood that the next
generation of Soviet leaders will be more willing to negotiate
than this one.

To this clearly unacceptable policy, Ulam juxtaposed a position
he termed "negotiating from a position of strength," which stressed
the weakened military position of the West and the proposition
that the West cannot successfully negotiate with the Soviet Union
unless and until the West achieves military parity again, especially
with respect to strategic weapons. The difficulty, as Ulam went on
to point out, is that military strength in and of itself hardly

constitutes a successful foreign policy, as is suggested by our
failure to take policy advantage of our enormous military superiority
over the Soviet Union at the close of World War II. Ulam concluded
by stressing that the United States will suffer a further deterioration in its position, unless the tremendous power of the West can
be mobilized and coordinated, unless the West can demonstrate that
"freedom and power go together."

For his part, Alexander Dallin presented a view espoused primarily by younger scholars who have trained at major American university graduate centers during the 1960s and 1970s and who have
participated in various Soviet-American exchange programs. This
more recent point of view maintains that one can truly understand
the Soviet Union only through proper social science graduate training, accompanied by field experience in the Soviet Union.

Dallin insisted that there are no instant solutions; that the
Soviet Union is a global power with which we have no choice but to
deal; that ideology is crucial to Soviet behavior abroad; and he
cast doubt upon the notion that the West can and must seek to make
the U.S.S.R. a responsible actor in the international arena through
various attempts at behavior modification. Dallin maintained that
Soviet-American relations are no longer a "zero-sum game" and that
both we and the Soviet population have more to gain than to lose
from contacts. Therefore, the major question that must be raised
concerning Soviet behavior abroad is what price will a Soviet
leadership be willing to pay in order to obtain any given policy
goal. Dallin argued that Washington must establish thresholds of
acceptable risk. Moreover, we need to develop a menu or price
list of Western actions, stating that if the Soviet Union takes
action "X" we will take action "Y". This schedule of rewards and
penalties must be consistently adhered to (something Dallin maintains has never really been done) and must be coordinated with
the efforts of our European allies. Dallin concluded by warning
that the loss of American influence in any given part of the world
should not be necessarily viewed as a Soviet gain.

Both speakers, then, offered summaries of well-established
positions within the U.S. Soviet-studies community, and managed
to agree on three points: (a) that it is in America's interest to
maintain a stable international environment; (b) that military
strength per se is not sufficient to guarantee American interests;
and (c) that coordinated and synchronized American-European actions
are a necessary step for dealing successfully with Soviet aggression.

One member of the audience noted that there was a broad agreement in the positions of both speakers. They both had a similar
view of what the policy issues are, although they arrived at that
view by differing paths. According to the questioner, Ulam was
essentially arguing that the United States does not press the
Soviets enough while Dallin was saying that, at times, the United
States may be pressing them too hard. Behind this difference of

degree lies a broad consensus that the American position should be
to press the Soviets. Both Ulam and Dallin agreed with this assess-
ment but did so by raising different points. Ulam suggested that
the real problem is not necessarily pressing the Soviets, but
having a clearer recognition of those Soviet behavior patterns that
are unacceptable. He noted that the United States has not been as
problematical a force on the world scene as the Soviet Union; he
wondered why we have not tried to make the Soviets pay a higher
price for some of their recent gains. Dallin also agreed with the
questioner, but took issue with Ulam on his definition of unacceptable Soviet behavior. Dallin indicated that the Soviet actions in
Iran and Ethiopia, for example, really were not very important
transgressions of the existing international order. While Afghanistan was different, Dallin continued, he, at least, did not take
the issue of the "Finlandization" of Europe as a serious threat.

A number of practical issues were raised during the discussion.
How can the United States get its allies to cooperate with it? Can
the United States really modify Kremlin behavior? What are the
American sticks, what are the carrots? Specific questions were
raised about Soviet behavior in Afghanistan, Ethiopia, Angola, and
Poland. Several members of the audience indicated that the United
States has neither carrots nor sticks sufficient to influence Soviet
behavior in any given part of the world. It was suggested that
real difficulties in Soviet-American relations arise not through
conscious Soviet aggression but through differing reactions by
American and Soviet policymakers to events neither has initiated
and neither controls. Under such circumstances the United States
cannot reach agreement with its own allies until an American consensus is achieved concerning national objectives.

EAST ASIA

U.S. NATIONAL ECONOMIC INTERESTS IN EAST ASIA

Hugh Patrick

Introduction

The purpose of this essay is to focus on U.S. national economic
interests in East Asia, as one important component of American
overall national interests both within the region and vis-a-vis
the entire world. Four interrelated issues are discussed: First,
what are American national economic interests in East Asia? Second,
what are the most important likely economic developments in the
region in the 1980s? Third, how should the United States respond
to these regional economic dynamics? Finally, how high should
U.S. economic interests in East Asia rank relative to those in
other regions and relative to domestic considerations? First,
however, it may be useful to explore briefly the interrelationships
among economic, political, and security variables.

A regional approach to national foreign policy issues is
appropriate. At the same time, perhaps for economic even more than
political and security relationships, American national interests
toward most regions of the world fit within quite explicit, relatively concrete global objectives. American interests are viewed
and handled at three levels: bilateral, regional, and global.
For economic interests relating to East Asia, to date the focus
has tended to be primarily either bilateral or global. I return
to this issue as we discuss the concept of region later.

It is obvious that American economic interests constitute an
important component of overall U.S. foreign policy interests.
However, this is often under-apppreciated. The "high road" of
military security-oriented grand strategy is often pursued without the understanding that fundamental economic forces are dramatically altering the world, and that these are (or at least should
be) forcing changes in strategic thinking. There is a mystique
that derives from strategic thinking because it is exciting and
enjoyable; it involves considerable speculation without sufficient

information, and it does not embody a deeply rigorous analytical framework. To strategic thinkers, it must often seem that economics is technical and dull. That does not mean, however, that economics is unimportant.

There is not space to develop in any detail examples where economic forces have changed the world and changed strategic relationships over the last quarter-century. Perhaps a few examples will be suggestive of the broader implications of economic forces at work. For example, it can be argued that the relative decline in U.S. global power is more economic in origin than political or military. Relatedly, the world has seen the flowering of the Industrial Revolution, first with the recovery of Western Europe, then with the rapid sustained growth of Japan, and more recently in the development of some 8-10 NICs (newly industrializing countries) in the world, including (in East Asia) South Korea, Taiwan, and Hong Kong. This industrialization process has brought about major changes in comparative advantage among specific industries in different countries, with relatively rapidly changing cost competitiveness and foreign trade flows. This has put pressure on those economies where important traditional industries are losing out. Because neither capital nor labor is very malleable, it takes time to shift them from declining industries to other, more productive uses, and this process is often painful and costly. The steel industry is one example. By the end of World War II the U.S. industry was the world leader in output, productivity, and cost competitiveness. Gradually the Japanese steel industry came to surpass the American industry. By the mid-1970s it was clearly not only very large, but the world's lowest-cost producer. Now, however, it is probably more efficient to build large-scale, integrated steel plants in first-tier developing countries where labor skills are adequate and wage rates are still relatively low. It is even more competitive if such countries also have their own inexpensive iron ore and/or coal reserves.

Another example of economic change that affects political and security relationships lies in the increasing scarcity of low cost energy, notably oil, which has been combined with the OPEC exercise of monopoly bargaining power. Over the past quarter-century the world economy, and especially the industrial economy, has come to depend increasingly upon oil in order to operate. As world oil supplies decline relative to growing demand, as political and other events cause sudden declines in oil production in selected countries, as OPEC raises prices, and as consuming nations are slow to respond, problems of the prices and quantities of oil and other energy supplies have become of paramount importance in both the short and longer runs. These obviously have had implications far beyond the economic, involving political and security relationships at their most fundamental levels. I return to this issue later.

In terms of U.S. foreign policy, several interrelated propositions are worthy of consideration. First, the linkage among broad economic interests, security interests, political interests, and indeed other national interests has become substantial; it is likely to become even more substantial in the future. Thus, a change in economic circumstances or in national economic policies will have important implications for other foreign policy objectives. For example, how well, or poorly, the United States manages its domestic economy will be central to its foreign policy objectives and their implementation. Thus, for example, American economic performance will significantly affect Japanese views of the reliability of the United States as an ally. Moreover, a change in political or military circumstances will affect American economic interests and the use of economic policy instruments to achieve other objectives. For example, trade embargoes have been utilized with Iran and with the U.S.S.R., following the development of the Iran hostage issue and the Afghanistan invasion. As a corollary, while linkage among broad economic and other variables is probably inevitable and often desirable, attempted linkage on specific small issues can well be dangerously counterproductive. To use economic jargon, while it may be a general-equilibrium world (in which all variables and their interrelationships must be considered), for many purposes -- for example, negotiating with Japan on textile quotas -- it probably is better to make partial-equilibrium assumptions (that everything else remains unchanged).

The second general proposition is that a major foundation of U.S. world leadership is America's central role in the maintenance of the international economic system of relatively free trade, payments, and capital flows. This used to be called the "liberal trading system," though perhaps it would be now more appropriate to call it the "conservative trading system." At any rate, regardless of terminology this system is indeed an essential feature of the American relationship with all the other market economies in the world, in other words, the entire world minus the Communist countries.

The third proposition is that the relative economic power of the United States will continue to decline, and this will put ever greater strains on America's ability and willingness to maintain its commitment to an open international economic order.

The American share of world GNP, approximately one-half at the end of World War II, has now declined to about one-quarter. The U.S. share of world trade has decreased to about one-eighth of the world total. In some sense these trends reflect the very success of past American foreign economic policy in encouraging the growth and development of Western Europe, Japan, the NICs, and indeed all developing countries. However, I do not feel we thought through adequately the implications of this process, what it means to shift from being a hegemonic economic power to simply the "first among equals." The United States continues to have the ability to veto changes in the rules of the international economic system, but no longer has the ability to impose unilaterally the rules or rule changes.

As a consequence of this decline in relative economic power, many Americans tend to feel frustrated over such matters as the decline in the value of the dollar, the ability of other countries to produce many products of high quality, and so forth. While there is a tendency to blame foreigners for American economic problems, there is also some perception of being "out-competed." It is not surprising that protectionist pressures have become increasingly strong. The problem, however, is that protectionism goes against the basic fabric of U.S. national interests, not only economically, but in terms of political and indeed strategic interests as well.

Two conclusions emerge from this analysis. First, any definition of, and thinking about, U.S. strategic interests must include economic variables and the interrelationships and feedback processes among economic, political, and security variables. It is my impression that economic variables are only inadequately incorporated into the thinking and analysis of American foreign policy makers and strategic thinkers. Second, U.S. world leadership -- which I assume to be one of the fundamental national interests -- is perhaps more likely to be undermined over the longer run by changing economic circumstances and inadequate economic policies than by changes in military or political dimensions. This conclusion is controversial; it merits discussion and debate.

What are U.S. national economic interests in East Asia?

First, it should be understood that U.S. national economic interests in East Asia are essentially identical to American foreign economic interests worldwide. These include:

a) rapid and stable growth of the East Asian economies;

b) a free, open, competitive, nondiscriminatory, multilateral system of trade, payments, and capital flows;

c) active American participation in this system of growth and economic interchange.

These objectives benefit American consumers and other users of imports, producers of exports, investors, and owners of technology. They are also essential to achieve the political and security objectives of a strong and beneficial American economic presence in the region.

At the same time it should be recognized that East Asia, even narrowly defined, is a very heterogeneous region. Moreover, U.S. economic interests have usually been seen through bilateral prisms, especially with Japan and China.

Before considering American regional economic interests more specifically, it may be useful to note several key features of the region itself. By a narrow geographical definition, East Asia consists of Japan, China, North Korea, South Korea, Taiwan, and Hong Kong. It is not clear that these economies comprise an economic region. China and North Korea have state-planned, Socialist economic systems; the others embody market-oriented, private enterprise, capitalist systems. China is huge in land and population; its natural resource base is huge in absolute terms, but not relative to its population. Japan is among the economically advanced, industrial nations, with a GNP/capita in 1978 of $7,280.[1] The NICs have successfully industrialized, with GNP/capita of $3,040 in Hong Kong, $1,400 in Taiwan, and $1,160 in South Korea. The two Communist states have low incomes -- $730 in North Korea, and $230 in China. The Chinese estimate is low, even at the official exchange rate used; a doubling would not be unreasonable, but even so, China is still underdeveloped and poor.

The East Asian economies vary immensely in total size. Japan's economy is huge, the third largest in the world, with a GNP of $836 billion in 1978, and about $1.2 trillion in 1980 as a consequence of growth, yen appreciation, and some inflation. By standard GNP measures, Japan's economy is as large as all the Asian-Pacific economies combined. China has a medium-large economy but it remains backward. The World Bank estimate of China's GNP in 1978 is $219 billion, about the same as Canada (which has one-fortieth the population). As noted, this estimate is low; nonetheless, a doubling means that Chinese GNP is only one-half that of Japan's, and only one-sixteenth in per capita terms. Nonetheless, relative to the other economies of the region, China is very large, about equal to all the developing economies of East and Southeast Asia combined. The other GNPs (in 1978) were: South Korea, $42.5 billion; Taiwan, $23.9 billion; Hong Kong, $14.1 billion; and North Korea, $12.5 billion. All the East Asian economies have grown quite rapidly for sustained periods. The average GNP growth rates for 1970-78 were: Japan, 5 percent; China, 6 percent; South Korea, 9.7 percent; Taiwan, 8 percent; Hong Kong, 8.2 percent; North Korea, 7.2 percent.

The sizes of the East Asian economies are only imperfect indicators of the U.S. economic involvement with them. There are major

[1]In order to obtain comparability, the basic data cited here are from the World Bank (World Development Report, 1980) and International Monetary Fund (Direction of Trade Yearbook, 1980).

differences in the share and importance of foreign trade and other kinds of foreign economic intercourse among these economies. Two-way merchandise trade is one measure of American economic interests vis-a-vis East Asia.

First, it is clear that the bilateral economic relationship with Japan overwhelms all other American economic interests in Asia. U.S. trade with Japan in 1979 amounted to $44 billion, and is estimated to be about $51 billion in 1980. Japan is not only where American economic interests are, it is where they will continue to be predominantly in Asia in the future. The United States should regard it as a high priority to maintain good economic relations with Japan, both on its own merits and because Japan is the major ally of the United States in Asia.

In contrast, U.S.-China trade is of minor importance to date. In 1979 it amounted to $2.3 billion; and it is estimated to approach $4 billion in 1980. This relatively minor economic interest is clearly subservient to and a part of American strategic and political interests vis-a-vis China. From China's point of view, the need for American technology and, to a lesser extent perhaps, American capital, will be very strong, as will its need for American food and cotton.

Third, U.S. trade with South Korea ($8.5 billion), Taiwan ($8.4 billion), and Hong Kong ($6.1 billion) is of substantial economic importance to the United States. Each is a significantly more important economic partner than China.

The United States has essentially no trade with North Korea. Even if North Korea and the United States were to alter their policies substantially, it is unlikely that bilateral trade would develop significantly. Thus, this economic relationship is likely to be less important than, say, the American economic relationship with Papua New Guinea. Accordingly, North Korea is not considered further.

The basic structure of American trade with the East Asian economies is shaped by respective comparative advantages. The East Asian economies produce and export manufactured goods (most are labor intensive in production), almost all of which compete directly with American producers in the U.S. market. While initially in textiles, apparel, and other similar labor-intensive manufactures, such as electrical consumer goods, over time the range and sophistication of East Asian exports to the United States has increased. As is well known, Japan has been in the vanguard of this structural transformation of the commodity composition of trade. While American consumers and users have benefited from the imports from East Asia, American producers in import-competing industries have been hurt, some of them seriously. Much of the protectionist pressure in the United States, as is discussed later, has emanated from the impact of imports from East Asia. As the first large-scale

exporter, Japan has borne much of the political brunt of opening
the American market. Subsequently Taiwan, South Korea, and Hong
Kong, and more recently China, have entered that market, but to a
considerable degree they have simply been replacing Japan's share
and have had to pay much less of a political price. At times,
however, the cumulative impact of trade in specific commodities
has increased substantially. Thus, the United States has over time
extended bilateral trade restrictions to the region as in earlier
textile quotas against Japan, and more recently in orderly marketing agreements on color televisions from Taiwan, South Korea, Hong
Kong, and Japan.

U.S. exports to East Asia have reflected American comparative
advantage in foodgrains, other land-based resources, high-technology
industrial items, and luxury consumer goods. On the whole, the
tendency has been for the United States to have bilateral trade
deficits with the East Asian market economies and surpluses with
China. This is primarily because they must import oil and other
raw materials as well as manufactures, and because their import
demand does not completely coincide with the U.S. export structure.
It should be recognized that bilateral trade imbalances are economically desirable. It would be economically very inefficient to
reduce bilateral trade to a balanced level based on the lower
limit. Indeed, that is the basic economic efficiency of the multilateral system of trade payments, and of viewing balance-of-payments
positions in global rather than bilateral terms. Nonetheless,
bilateral trade deficits with the region, particularly with Japan,
have been (mistakenly and inappropriately) political issues in
the United States.

In sum, American economic interests in Asia focus mainly on
Japan, secondarily on the NICs, and only tertiarily and relatively
unimportantly on China.

What are likely developments in East Asia in the 1980s?

The simple answer to this question is: more of the same.

First, the growth rates of the East Asian economies will probably be above world averages. Relatively, then, this will be a
region of rapid growth. Japan will have the most rapid growth
rate among the major OECD industrial nations. I (perhaps optimis-
tically) project a 6 percent real GNP growth rate for Japan on
average for the decade of the 1980s, unless the world environment
seriously deteriorates. While each of the other East Asian economies will have its own problems, on the whole they are likely to
do quite well. The World Bank projects that East and Southeast Asia
will be the fastest growing regions in the world. The growth rate
of the Chinese economy is the most difficult to predict. While
there are many problems, China may well be able to achieve growth
at a 5-6 percent rate. The constraints on Chinese growth are

essentially domestic, unlike the rest of the region. It is an inefficient, poorly organized economy that lacks infrastructure.
On the other hand it has high savings and investment rates, and is
going through an interesting period of economic reforms and increasing openness to the world economy. It probably will have substantial balance-of-payments problems during the course of the
decade. However, the Soviet experience indicates that an economy
can grow rapidly by investing at a high rate, even if inefficiently,
over time.

Second, for the market economies of the region, the major constraints on economic growth will emanate from external sources.
These will be mainly the direct and indirect effects of rises in
oil prices, especially if there are sudden sharp surges in prices.
The greatest operational threat to the world economy is a major,
sustained interruption of oil supplies, essentially a Middle East
issue. For the Japanese such a cutoff of oil supplies is a catastrophic fear, roughly equivalent to the American gut fear of nuclear
attack by the Soviet Union.

Third, trade in the region will grow at least as fast as GNP,
probably more rapidly. Accordingly, this will be a region of rapid
trade growth, providing both opportunities for and pressures on
the American economy. One significant issue is the degree to which
China will become more foreign trade oriented, in its ability both
to absorb imports and to generate exports. Development of Chinese
oil and coal will require substantial foreign involvement; export
of labor-intensive manufactures is also likely to require considerable foreign involvement. Substantial American and Japanese capital and technology flows to China seem likely.

Fourth, economic interaction among the economies of the region
is likely to increase relatively as well as absolutely, and perhaps
to become more intense as a result. Institutionally this will continue to lead to greater interest in the possibilities of arrangements for regional economic cooperation, especially among the market
economies. In this context the definition of "region" becomes important economically and politically.

East Asia does not seem to be much of an economic region. To
be a significant economic region probably requires a substantial
number of economies actively involved in foreign trade, in practice
meaning market-oriented, capitalist-oriented economies. An Asian
economic region would need to include, in addition to Japan, South
Korea, Taiwan, and Hong Kong, at the minimum the ASEAN countries of
Southeast Asia. Even this is probably too narrow. Oceania should
be included; essentially this means Australia, plus a number of
small economies. Australia, with its immense natural resources and
increasing trade relationships in Asia, is insufficiently understood and appreciated in the United States.

An even broader view would define the Asian-Pacific region to
include the other major Pacific economies, namely the United States,
Canada, and increasingly Mexico. Since the early 1970s, American
trade with this more broadly defined Asian-Pacific region has been
greater than with Europe. To be sure, most of it has been with
Japan (excluding Canada from this measurement). Excluding Canada,
U.S. trade with the Pacific Basin countries in 1979 amounted to
$97.6 billion, 45 percent with Japan, and 70 percent with the East
Asia region as narrowly defined.

One consequence of this increasing degree of specific economic
interaction and economic interdependence has been rising interest
in the formation of a Pacific economic community, or similar
regional economic institutional arrangements. This is not merely
a discussion among academics, but in the last two years has become
a matter of consideration by governments. It probably will take
considerable time before any institutional arrangements develop.
Politically, institutional progress depends essentially upon ASEAN
support and even leadership. However, even short of that we can
expect substantial ad hoc governmental discussions and cooperation on a number of regional-specific economic and perhaps other
issues, without the United States necessarily being included.

How should the United States respond to these regional economic dynamics?

First, the United States should recognize that there are many economic forces in the region about which it can do little. For
example, while American policies can certainly influence trade
flows between the United States and East Asia, there is little it
can do about intra-regional trade flows. Similarly, much of the
impetus to economic growth emanates from domestic forces.

Nonetheless, there are important contributions the United
States can make to the dynamic processes of GNP and trade growth.
Perhaps the most important lie in the arena of energy supplies and
prices. Energy is a global problem. What the United States does,
and what it and Japan do together, will be important for the entire
world, especially East Asia. A whole range of steps must be taken
to hold down rises in the cost of energy, to minimize interruptions of supply and, where they occur, to minimize the destruc-
tiveness of their impact. I regard energy problems as potentially
the most serious -- not only for the international economic system,
but in their political and security implications -- facing the United
States and indeed the world in the decade of the 1980s. Since the
East Asian market economies are particularly deficient in domestic
oil and other energy resources, this is an especially severe problem. American leadership thus is of great importance. The development of Chinese energy resources -- oil and coal -- for export
as well as domestic purposes should probably be among the highest
priorities of not only China but the United States and Japan as well.

An improved and stable American economic performance will benefit not only the United States but East Asia as well as the rest of the world. The United States is a very important market and source of supply for the region. It is a significant source of world growth of demand. Japan, too, plays an important role in this respect.

The United States should accommodate, and take advantage of, the basically healthy economic trends of the East Asia region. The United States needs to gear up in order to compete effectively in these growing markets, by increasing exports of goods, services, capital, and technology. Similarly, the United States should maintain a liberal import policy, that is, to continue to maintain East Asian access to American markets. In other words, the United States should become increasingly export oriented, not import restrictive. Incidentally, it should be noted that the share of exports in U.S. GNP doubled during the decade of the 1970s, as did the share of imports. Thus, while the United States can and should do more, it has already demonstrated that it is capable of responding to export opportunities as they develop.

The United States should be involved in discussions on any regional economic institutional arrangements in which the United States might potentially participate. There is a substantial cost to the United States in being left out, political even more than economic. It is in American interests to shape any institutions that may develop so that they do not become restrictive and undercut the global liberal economic system. Moreover, institutional arrangements are likely to offer positive opportunities to handle some of the regional economic (and other) problems more effectively, and are likely to provide a more limited regional vehicle for approaching global problems that do not yet seem capable of global solutions.

How high should U.S. economic interests in East Asia rank?

First, it should be stressed that overall U.S. economic interests in East Asia are not in conflict with American economic interests in other regions in the world. They are all part of a global economic strategy based on maintenance and reinforcement of an established international economic system. Thus, American regional economic interests in East Asia reinforce rather than conflict with interests in other regions.

At the same time it should be recognized that one major area of potential conflict is between oil-producing and oil-consuming nations. Moreover, there are potential conflicts in the event of a substantial oil shortage among the oil-consuming nations scrambling for supplies. This is essentially a U.S.-Japan story, in terms of the region. There are major opportunities for comprehensive cooperation in energy between the United States and Japan.

This is also the area of greatest potential conflict between the
two nations. It appears that despite the IEA neither country has
planned adequately for the possibility of a serious interruption
and shortfall of oil supplies, even unilaterally much less bi-
laterally, and that in a real crisis each could well pursue "beggar
thy neighbor" policies. This is probably the greatest threat to the
U.S.-Japan alliance in the 1980s.

Second, most Americans underestimate the economic benefit to
the United States of its economic relationships with the East Asian
region and more broadly the Asia-Pacific region. The United States
does not have broad-based expertise in government, business, or
academe on the Asia-Pacific region. Americans tend to be "Euro-
centric." Policymakers tend to think in military-security terms
rather than in terms of economic relationships. East Asia (and the
Asia-Pacific region) is not high in the consciousness of American
policymakers or those who influence policy. This should be reme-
died.

Third, to date much of the competitive pressure on specific
American industries over the past two decades has emanated from
East Asia. First it was Japan; this continues and will continue.
More recently it has been South Korea, Taiwan, and Hong Kong. Most
recently it has been China. It took two years to negotiate a minor
textile quota agreement with China because of the conflict between
domestic and foreign interests, economic as well as political. In
a sense East Asia has often been the source of the classic domestic
confrontation in the definition of U.S. national interests between
consumers, other import users, and producers of exports on the one
hand, and producers of import-competing goods on the other hand.
While the liberal American foreign trade policy has been fundamentally maintained, it has been chipped away here and there. Probably
perceptions abroad concerning U.S. protectionist trends are unduly
pessimistic. Nonetheless, there are real fears in East Asia as
elsewhere that the United States will abandon its liberal trade
position, not necessarily by a general change in policy, but by
sliding into ad hoc protectionism.

East Asia is likely to continue to be the major cutting edge
of foreign competitive pressure on many American industries. A
significant danger is that, in trying to solve specific industry
problems on an ad hoc basis through a series of deals with these
countries as has been done in the past, the United States will
indeed become protectionist. This would be disastrous for U.S.
foreign policy and for the world. It would put the United States
in the position of no longer being the champion of the international economic system it has spent the last 35 years building
and maintaining. In this sense, East Asia is likely to be the
lightning rod for the U.S. choice between protectionism and world
economic leadership.

PERSPECTIVES ON U.S. POLICIES IN ASIA DURING THE 1980s

Robert A. Scalapino

Since World War II, East Asia (and certainly Western Europe) has
been a region of first priority for American foreign policy. The
reasons are obvious: whether the measurements be economic, political,
cultural, or strategic, that half of the world we call the Pacific-
Asian area is of vital significance to the American future. I
would assume that two additional areas will bulk large in American
concern during the 1980s, namely, the Middle East and the long-
neglected Western Hemisphere. And certainly U.S.-U.S.S.R. relations will be of critical importance globally. But politics is
increasingly becoming a seamless web. Relations with the U.S.S.R.
relate directly to Asia, as do those with the Arabs.

What are current interests in Asia, and how should we plan for
their fulfillment? At the outset, it is essential to distinguish
certain general considerations, region-specific concerns, and
single-country requirements. In truth, we have never had a Pacific-
Asian policy because we have never been able to integrate specific,
sometimes divergent bilateral and subregional policies. It is
time to rectify this deficiency by seeking to establish and maintain
the linkages that will add up to a coherent regional policy, and
by tying this policy to policies pursued elsewhere.

In the most basic terms, our interests in Asia can be divided
into three categories. Strategically, a broad equilibrium must be
maintained in the Pacific-Asian area, a power balance preventing
the dominance or threat of dominance by any single nation over the
region. This requires multilateral security responsibilities to a
much greater extent than currently exist. It also necessitates
greater attention to the economic, political, and social issues confronting Asian societies because security starts at home, and the
connection between targets of opportunity and external intervention is an all too obvious fact of our times.

Politically, the American interest lies in seeing all societies
in the region progress toward greater openness, not only because this
is consonant with our values, but because such states allow a

greater flow of international communications of all types, with the
risks of fanaticism or paranoia thereby reduced. If political
openness and advances in human rights are to ensue, the struggle
to institutionalize politics must be gradually advanced. Yet it is
more important that the American government and people recognize
that foreign models cannot be applied mechanically to societies
that have different cultural heritages as well as different current
needs and capacities. There are real political and economic alternatives for Asian nations, but neither Western-style parliamentarism
nor Soviet-style communism is likely to prevail in its pure form,
and American policies must be adjusted to that fact.

In economic terms, the U.S. interest lies in advancing regional
economic intercourse to the maximum extent, resisting protectionism,
and working with others to reduce the North-South economic gap. The
steady development of Asia's poorer societies is, on balance, a necessary concomitant of peace and stability. Moreover, the opportunities for progress in economic development are greater in Asia than
in most other parts of the so-called Third World.

Having set forth American interests in their broadest dimensions, we must turn briefly to the American domestic scene. The
very first requirement for an effective American foreign policy
in any region today is to get our domestic economy in order. Credible foreign policies will stem only from successful domestic policies. As long as our people are deeply troubled by an assortment
of economic and social ills, they cannot be expected to participate in the construction of any new international order with great
ardor.

In the process of tackling domestic problems, it is also important to rebuild a sense of confidence, cohesion, and pride in
America. In the recent past, we have concentrated too heavily
upon our various divisions and our supposed shortcomings. If what
we have denominated "liberalism" is currently laboring under a
cloud of suspicion, it is partly because of the burden of self-
doubt and self-guilt in which so many "liberals" have wallowed.
We need a rebirth of American nationalism, and this can be done
without succumbing to vulgarity or chauvinism if the task is not
left to the ultras.

We also need a more complex process of internal communications
across the diverse communities into which we have been cast as members of a highly differentiated society. In the arena of foreign
policy, for example, government, business, labor, academia, and the
media should interact on a far more frequent and effective basis.

Turning to the Pacific-Asian region, three general and interrelated prescriptions are in order. First, in strategic terms, our
security and a general equilibrium in Asia hinge upon two factors:
a continuing alignment with the major states that lie off the Asian
mainland, together with nations immediately related to the security

of such states; and secondly, the continued separation of the
People's Republic of China from any close alignment with the U.S.S.R.

The first factor requires a sustained defense relationship with
Japan, the Republic of Korea, Taiwan (assuming no peaceful unification with the People's Republic of China), the ASEAN (Association of
Southeast Asian Nations) community, Australia, and New Zealand.
Clearly, the precise relation must vary with the country concerned,
but the Guam Declaration of 1969 should set the general terms of
the American commitment. Primary responsibility for defense must
rest with the nation immediately involved and include the requirement
of setting one's own house in order. In case of need, moreover,
American military support should take the form of weapons transfer
together with air and naval assistance. The dispatch of large-scale
expeditionary forces is not feasible.

Beyond setting forth the nature of the American commitment, it
is essential to take burden sharing in this field seriously. Some
states are engaged in major efforts, but others -- and most notably
Japan -- remain essentially dependent upon the United States despite
their economic capacity for a much more extensive effort and their
great stake in a secure Pacific-Asian region.

In the years ahead, Japan should undertake the following security responsibilities. First, Japan's role in sea and air defense
should be extended over the West and South Pacific. The Japanese
government has already officially stated that it is legally possible, under the present Constitution, to defend Japanese vessels
on the high seas, and the Japanese Maritime Self-Defense Force is
now committed to a target of assuring the security of waters for
several hundred nautical miles from Japanese coasts as well as
sea routes serving Japan for up to 1,000 nautical miles from Japan.
It remains, however, to develop a naval and air force fully capable
of undertaking these responsibilities, and this cannot be done
under present financial provisions for the self-defense force.

Second, there is a need for two separate, informal consultative Northeast Asian panels on defense-related issues. The first
should involve South Korea, the United States, and Japan; the second,
the People's Republic of China, the United States, and Japan. Some
bilateral discussions between Japan and all of the above parties
have taken place, but it is appropriate to regularize and broaden
the contacts. The functions of these panels should be confined
for the present to the exchange of information, including political
security assessments. Yet operating in this manner, the panels
could serve the vital function of keeping all parties abreast of
current developments, and represent the type of cooperation feasible
under present circumstances. Meanwhile, Japan's participation in
joint defense planning and military exercises with the United
States, currently under way, should be continued and expanded.

The ultimate decisions relating to Japan's security role in the 1980s naturally rest with the Japanese people; their perception of threat and the issue of American credibility will be key factors in the decisions that will be reached. At present, the prospects are for incremental rather than dramatic moves in the security realm. Under certain circumstances, however, Japan must be prepared to assume a larger role in the defense of neighboring states. It is not inconceivable that later developments may require Japan to pledge joint military assistance with the United States in the event of an external attack upon South Korea or Taiwan, while also pledging support for any peaceful unification of Korea and China-Taiwan. This would require some revision of Article Nine of the Japanese Constitution, which is not immediately feasible. Both the leaders and the people of Japan, however, know that their stake in a peaceful Northeast Asia is far greater than that of any other external power, including the United States. The present imbalance in security costs and risks is not going to be acceptable to the American people for the indefinite future. This is not to denigrate recent Japanese efforts, which, in comparison with the NATO nations, have been appreciable. Nevertheless, we are far from a satisfactory distribution of security burdens, and that fact must be faced squarely.

Under present circumstances, meanwhile, American military assistance to the Republic of Korea and to Taiwan should continue. In the case of South Korea, the presence of American troops remains as vital a symbol of the American commitment as does the presence of such troops in West Europe, and it serves to preserve the peace in this volatile region. Defensive military aid to Taiwan is also warranted as the ultimate status of that island evolves, both as a firm indication that the United States does not abandon viable states aligned with it and as an impetus toward a peaceful resolution of China-Taiwan relations.

ASEAN will continue to be essentially a consultative and economic body, yet in the face of Vietnam's disruption of regional peace that organization has taken political positions bearing strong security overtones, with each ASEAN member involved also in various forms of bilateral cooperation in the security realm. That will continue and should be encouraged.

At the same time, all parties must recognize that the security of these states hinges in the first instance upon progress -- on the economic, social, and political fronts at home -- sufficient to bolster internal cohesion and the legitimacy of the existing government. The external threat currently existing is primarily to Thailand. Here, the dual pledges of the People's Republic of China and the United States to support the Thai in the event of an attack should suffice to give Hanoi pause. But in Thailand as elsewhere, the front line in terms of security lies with the economy, and with the type of political and social policies that will provide the government with a broader base of support. Thus, there and in other

ASEAN states as well, the American contribution to security can be significant only if it encompasses developmental needs.

On the South Asian subcontinent, the U.S. strategic commitment should be strictly limited. For the near term at least, India will continue its alignment with the U.S.S.R. This need not be considered dangerous, because India is too large and too complex to be controlled by any external force, and it is entirely possible that various major changes will occur in the course of the next decade, upheavals beyond the control of the Soviet Union or any other power. In Pakistan also, the probabilities of instability are high, rendering external assistance on a large scale a dubious policy. A strong case can be made for providing military assistance to the Afghan resistance movement. This policy could be conducted unofficially, in the same manner as Soviet assistance is provided under comparable circumstances. One worrisome problem in the area is the growing likelihood of nuclear proliferation. An effort at U.S.-U.S.S.R. cooperation should be renewed, since on this issue we have mutual interests.

Turning to the second aspect of U.S. security interests in Asia, the integrity and independence of China will continue to be a matter of vital consequence in the years ahead. Here, a division of external labor is important. Under present conditions, there are good reasons why the United States should not engage in weapons sales to the People's Republic of China. The United States is in a unique position vis-a-vis the U.S.S.R., the world's other superpower. American arms sales to the People's Republic of China would be construed by Moscow and others as the final step of military alignment, the construction of a semi-permanent anti-Soviet bloc. All U.S.-U.S.S.R. negotiations would be rendered vastly more difficult if not impossible, and we would reenter the Cold War under conditions far more dangerous than in the late 1940s, to the great apprehension of our European and Japanese allies. It is vital to understand that, at present, the strengthening of the NATO and U.S.-Japan security alliances is dependent on the one hand upon an American policy of raising its total strength (economic and political, as well as military) and credibility, and on the other hand upon pursuing negotiations with the U.S.S.R. in all earnestness. That there should be equally serious responsibilities on the part of America's allies is one of the central themes of this essay, but unless the United States is prepared to accept the dual path sketched above, the current alliances will be in ever greater jeopardy (assuming, of course, no catastrophic Soviet move such as military intervention in Poland, which might precipitate the need for major shifts in U.S., Japanese, and European policies).

An American military alignment with the People's Republic of China under present circumstances has another serious weakness. If it is conceived as an ongoing, steadily expanding relationship -- as would seem natural, viewed from Beijing's perspective, especially in light of the progression thus far -- it will not only render American policy toward the Soviet Union less flexible, but it will also involve the United States in rising commitments to the security of China without the requisite increases in the capacity to fulfill such commitments. China's military capabilities will remain essentially defensive for the foreseeable future, and neither Japan nor Western Europe is prepared to play a significant security role on behalf of China at this point. On the other hand, if military alignment with China is a ploy to induce better Soviet behavior, and is frozen or reduced in the event of such a response, then the People's Republic of China will be rightfully angered, having reason to doubt American sincerity.

The arguments against U.S. arms sales to China do not necessarily apply to Japan and West Europe. The broad strategic position of these countries is not the same as that of the United States. There is no present indication, however, that the People's Republic of China is interested in extensive arms purchases from any source. The priorities are currently upon building an economic infrastructure and improving the public livelihood while maintaining the old strategy of joint reliance upon a nuclear deterrent and modified "people's war," deferring large-scale conventional military modernization to a later point. This is a sound policy, and if it can be sustained, the People's Republic of China will have a greater overall strength in the middle-term future than if the concentration were immediately upon a massive military buildup.

In the final analysis, China's security today depends less upon a military alignment with the United States, and more upon the capacity and will of the United States to serve as a global balance to Soviet power. As in the case of the ASEAN states, moreover, the security of the People's Republic of China is inextricably connected with the success or failure of the economic modernization program, and it is in this area that the United States, together with other Western nations and Japan, should make the primary contributions. In any case, moreover, one vital fact should never be overlooked: security issues relating to China are strategic issues that concern Japan, the ASEAN states, and West Europe; American policies in this realm should be based upon a consensus of these parties.

In sum, the Pacific-Asian region is likely to see the continuance of two loosely constructed blocs in the period immediately ahead. A U.S.-Japan-South Korea-People's Republic of China/Taiwan-ASEAN-Pakistan group will confront a Soviet-Outer Mongolia-(North Korea?)-Vietnam-India group. Obviously, these blocs do not represent firm alliances, and within them certain contradictions and potential conflicts exist. In a few cases, moreover, a contest for allegiance ensues. One of the most basic political trends on the international front at present is the movement from alliance to alignment. Working with aligned states -- seeking to consult with and in varying ways strengthen them while negotiating with members of the adversary group, differentiating treatment depending on their behavior -- is the central U.S. task of the 1980s in this region.

Meanwhile, at the political level, several issues must be confronted. One question is the degree of importance to be assigned human rights in the construction and execution of American foreign policy. Here, certain facts must be faced. As indicated earlier, the prospects in Asia for political liberalism of a classic Western type are not good for the period immediately ahead. Japan excepted, most Pacific-Asian states will operate as quasi-authoritarian systems at best. In this setting, the American dilemma has been well exemplified by the difficulties the Carter administration has faced in effectuating its much-heralded human rights policies. Launched in an effort to provide a moral foundation for American foreign policy and, hopefully, to rebuild an American consensus, human rights criteria have proven impossible to apply uniformly, as should have been expected. There can be no single test for an American commitment, but considerations of global or regional balance will always demand high priority.

Does this mean that the American concern over human rights should be abandoned, at least as an official instrument used in formulating foreign policy? The answer, in my opinion, is in the negative -- but with certain important qualifications. It should never be forgotten that, for better or worse, the American people have always insisted upon some ethical or moral foundation for U.S. foreign policy, and this demand will not disappear. We are not Europeans. What is needed, however, is a far more sophisticated delineation of performance among the many political societies that make up the global community, and one paying some homage to cultural and developmental diversity.

To demand that emerging societies conform to American-style. liberalism is both unrealistic and ethnocentric. There is an important distinction to be made, however, between quasi-authoritarian, pluralistic societies and fully authoritarian states dedicated to monolithism and a one-party dictatorship. All societies harbor changes within them, but the chances for political evolution are generally better in the former type of state. Until such distinctions have been carefully drawn, and criteria for judging advances and retrogression have been refined, "human rights" will be less useful and less moral than its ardent adherents claim. Once these tasks have been accomplished, however, it will be easier to sustain our legitimate concerns: underwriting and advancing such international declarations as the Helsinki Convention.

How should human rights relate to our relations with specific societies in the Pacific-Asian region? It ought to be acknowledged that our political ties with the fully open societies -- Japan, Australia, and New Zealand -- have special significance. In a number of states, including Malaysia, Thailand, and Indonesia, progress toward greater political openness has been made. This should be

officially praised. Today, our concerns focus upon South Korea,
and in this instance, we should combine a firmness of commitment to
the Korean people with strong private counsel to the government
against those repressive actions that can and will influence American public and congressional opinion. Societies like Korea face
ups and downs in their struggle to modernize politically and establish institutions suitable to Korean culture. Indeed, a widespread
problem in Asia today lies in the weakness of political institutions
and hence, the high degree of dependence upon personalized politics.

With respect to this and related problems, it would be highly
appropriate at this point if Americans in the private sector were to
initiate an ongoing collaboration with Asians to explore the broadest issues relating to political and economic institutions designed
for the future. Such an exploration could take place in the form
of a permanent study group involving some rotation of membership,
and including academic, professional, business, and labor representatives. In order to be productive, it would require a long-term
existence, with earlier studies, theses, and recommendations periodi-
cally reviewed. Engaged in the commissioning of research on critical issues, including in its membership representatives of Pacific-
Asian societies on a cross-cultural, cross-developmental, cross-
ideological basis, it would naturally provide for differences of
interpretation and policy recommendation. Yet, it would also en-
able a focus upon the most basic organizational questions of the
coming decades.

In the final analysis, of course, organizational issues --
however vital -- cannot be divorced from ideological considerations.
In most societies at present, the trend has been toward pragma-
tism, toward an ad hoc experimentation to see what will work. As
a result, ideology in its classic forms has declined. That is both
understandable and, in some respects, desirable. Yet it is now
clear that when values appear to be abandoned, the citizenry ultimately becomes confused, listless, or dispirited. Something will
arise to fill the vacuum, and currently we are witnessing the renewed potency of religious ideology -- moving forward in politics
in the face of a secular ideological retreat. Christianity, Islam,
Judaism, and even Buddhism are reasserting themselves in the political arena.

Once again, the basic issue of ideology -- its role in and its
consequences for the modern society -- warrants attention via some
type of cross-cultural study group drawn from the private sector.
To probe the basic issues of political organization and ideology
is to raise the most fundamental questions pertaining to the future
of all societies. At a point when the instrumentalities of destruction are so advanced, it is essential that we commence the enormously complex task of addressing the long-term issues of political
structure and substance across cultural and developmental lines.
This is not a task of governments but of key elites. Yet it is an
ever more essential complement to intergovernmental relations.

It remains to discuss briefly the economic element in U.S.
Asian policy. Here, the first requirement is to be fully realistic.
The age of large-scale, unilateral American economic assistance is
over. As in the security arena, the premium will be upon a genuine
multilateralism, a fuller sharing of responsibilities.

One of the paradoxes with which we must wrestle in the years
ahead is the one between the spectacular rise of economic interdependence on the one hand, and the increasing potency of economic nationalism on the other hand. The latter movement involves most advanced industrial societies at least as much as the late-developing
countries. If it is to be contained, domestic economies will have
to be improved, and as noted earlier, that is the first requirement
for the United States. But beyond this, if the American people are
to be attracted to any new commitment to economic internationalism,
a forceful symbol of the commitment of others is necessary. This
is the central political reason why the quest for some type of
Pacific Basin community must be continued, indeed, accelerated.
Progress will probably be slow, at least as it pertains to concrete
organizational form. Various obstacles are to be overcome, including those relating to membership, function, and structure. But in
the broadest sense, regionalism -- in a wide variety of forms --
is the wave of the future. The nation-state will remain the most
basic socioeconomic and political unit through the 20th century
and beyond. And for certain purposes, global efforts will be most
appropriate. Yet there is a steadily increasing rationale for
intermediate organizations, particularly of an economic nature, as
science and technology change every aspect of relations among neighboring societies.

In the meantime, three considerations should play a major role
in American economic and cultural policies toward the Pacific-Asian
region. First, adjustments on both sides are essential if an intensified U.S.-Japanese economic conflict is to be avoided. Indeed,
some short-term American protectionist measures seem almost inevitable. In the middle and long term, however, the health of the
American economy will be the key determinant, and Japan is in a
position to assist in a favorable outcome, albeit with the chief
responsibility lying with the American government and people. Meanwhile, we should seek closer coordination with Japan in matters
relating to broader economic policies for the Pacific-Asian region
as a whole.

Secondly, we are in a position to assist in a sizable transfer
of scientific and technological knowledge, and this can play a
major role in advancing relations between the United States and the
People's Republic of China, as well as those with other late-developing countries of Asia. The thousands of Asian students currently
in the United States represent a vital investment in the future,
one that is relatively inexpensive for the United States in comparison with its potential return.

There is one final requirement if America's Asian policies are
to be more effective. In recent times, we have woefully neglected
to provide for the expertise in our own nation that will be essential if we are to come abreast of the complex problems of the present and future. It is ironic that our substantial commitment to
the training of Asians is not matched by the training of Americans.
Foreign-language instruction in the Asian field is minimal, and not
progressing. Funds for research have shrunk, and we have only a
handful of major research institutes, none of them properly supported financially. Only a tiny number of specialists are able to
devote themselves to extensive research on contemporary Asia --
far fewer than is the case with the U.S.S.R. Governmental area experts are also few in number. For a relatively small expenditure
of funds, these deficiencies could be corrected, and the gains for
American policies would be far greater than those achieved by any
comparable expenditure.

DISCUSSION

U.S. NATIONAL INTERESTS IN EAST ASIA

The principal disagreement between Hugh Patrick and Robert Scalapino
concerned the attitude the United States should take toward Japan's
future defense commitment.

Scalapino urged that Japan take "burden sharing" seriously,
that Japanese naval units assume responsibility for the Pacific
and for the defense of oil delivery routes, and that Japan build up
its naval and air forces, even if this were to require, eventually,
an amendment of Article Nine of the Japanese Constitution. Patrick
argued that it would be unwise to urge upon the Japanese government
a course of action for which there is little Japanese popular
support and that would have high domestic political costs in Japan;
a better policy would be to suggest an increased Japanese economic
contribution to other goals, such as the maintenance of American
defense forces, accelerated economic development in China, involvement in projects that might assist stabilization in the Middle
East or Southeast Asia, and so forth. Japan should be expected to
bear a higher share of the economic burden, rather than to undertake
a serious rearmament program in the near future. Scalapino did
not believe that such a trade-off would be politically acceptable
in the United States. Patrick and others pointed out that Japanese
rearmament might well raise anxieties in Asia, where memories of
Japanese aggression still remain.

A second difference of emphasis centered on the position of
China. Patrick felt that China could not play a larger role in
Asia until it developed its economy, although it was pointed out
that China has already taken on a good deal of "burden sharing"
by tying down 40 Soviet divisions on its northern border. While
neither speaker thought U.S. arms sales to China advisable, Scalapino did suggest that the Europeans need not be so constrained.
Both the United States and Japan should invest technical and economic assistance in China's development, and Scalapino suggested
that joint defense discussions (United States, Japan, People's
Republic of China) would also be desirable.

Speakers in the audience pointed forcefully to the fundamental interest of the United States in preventing domination of
Asia by any other power, a policy of "anti-hegemonism" against
any coalition of forces that would push the United States off the
periphery of Asia. Most of the audience shared the view that the
best route to accomplish such a goal is a defensive multilateralism, through which the United States would maintain its alignment
with Japan, the Republic of Korea, Taiwan, ASEAN, Australia, and
New Zealand, and to some degree, the People's Republic of China.
Two questions, however, divided the audience: What is an acceptable
role for the Soviet Union as an Asian power? and to what degree
should the Western powers make a concerted effort to lure India
out of the Soviet orbit? It was observed that any addition to
world energy supplies is a net gain for all, and that Japan's
development of Siberian natural gas should be encouraged, even at
the cost of a modest increase in Japanese dependence upon it.
Second, India, as the world's largest democracy, should not be
assumed to be hostile to U.S. interests, although Mrs. Gandhi's
attitude does not make assistance easy. We should encourage others
to try to reduce the tensions between China and India.

It was agreed that the Pacific Basin community is a region of
great importance to the United States -- from the economic point of
view it is of equal importance with Europe. There is likely to be
relative equilibrium and continued economic growth in the region,
but the very strength of the region -- especially among the newly
industrializing countries -- is likely to produce conflicts within
the United States. East Asia will probably not produce the flash-
points of international crisis -- that role seems destined to be
played by the Middle East -- but East Asia may be the test of the
United States' commitment to the world trading system it has maintained since 1945.

LATIN AMERICA

THE UNITED STATES AND LATIN AMERICA IN THE 1980s

Constantine C. Menges

I THE U.S. NATIONAL INTEREST

More than 350 million people live in the 50 nations and soon-to-
be-independent territories of Latin America (including the Caribbean). During the next decade two entirely different sets of historical forces will be competing: on the positive side there is the
return to constitutional government in four nations, steps toward
continued political liberalization in others such as Brazil, along
with two decades of overall economic growth and rising living stan-
dards for many despite a doubling in population since 1960. The destructive trends include the severe economic threats posed by past
oil-price rises and possible future jumps, mounting inflation,
underemployment, and the recent slowdown in economic growth rates,
along with a resurgence of Cuban-supported terrorism, propaganda,
and political destabilization by the extreme left, with a corollary
increase in counterterror by the extreme right. The wisdom of
Latin American leaders and U.S. policy during the first years of
this decade may well be decisive in determining whether the positive
or the destructive trends shape the future history of the region.

     Latin America is often perceived as a region of economic
underdevelopment and poverty where the grand ideals of the Alliance
for Progress failed. In fact, like many vague perceptions this is
partially true, especially in terms of political development, but
also quite out of date, particularly in economic progress. For
the past 30 years the Latin American economies have been growing
at an average annual rate of 5.2 percent. Until the 1979 oil-
price shock, this growth rate had increased steadily each decade.
In per capita terms, this has meant a real average annual increase
of 2.7 percent, a rate of improvement that matches most industrial
nations and is higher than the Alliance for Progress target set in
1961. In most countries living conditions have improved for a
majority of the population. Signs of this include the visibly
expanded ownership of consumer goods and social improvements.
During the last 30 years, for example, life expectancy has increased
from less than 50 years to 62 years; there was a near-doubling in

primary school attendance from 55 percent of the age group to 90
percent and an increase in secondary school attendance from 10 percent to 35 percent, while university enrollment grew from 2 percent
of the age group to 9 percent. Contrary to the widespread impression,
the terms of trade for the region have improved steadily even for
countries that do not export oil. Exports have increased dramatically
and nearly all governments have operational control over their basic
exports (e.g., Mexico, Venezuela, Peru - oil, Chile - copper).

Despite this overall success in economic growth, the sharp
increase in population since 1960 (3.2 percent annually, the world's
second fastest) and the failure to redistribute economic gains more
equally have left significant proportions of the population in
poverty within most of the countries. In Mexico and Brazil, for
example, 30-40 percent of the population is estimated to live in
poverty, and similar or larger proportions hold for many though
not all of the countries.

Latin America recovered more quickly than expected from the
1973 fourfold increase in OPEC prices partly because of massive
borrowing from private and public lending institutions in the industrial democracies. This meant that annual foreign borrowing went
up from $3 billion in 1970 to $15 billion in 1975 to more than
$40 billion in 1980. The combined external debt of Brazil and
Mexico now totals more than $100 billion, and debt service requires
large proportions of their foreign exchange earnings.

Economic growth in Latin America has meant that it now is
the third largest market for U.S. products, following Europe and
Canada. These U.S. exports and imports totaled $50 billion in
1979 while U.S. private investment added up to $37 billion, or 20
percent of the worldwide total. At present, the United States
imports a number of strategically important minerals from Latin
America, including nearly 20 percent of its petroleum. Mexico,
Guatemala, and Venezuela also are estimated to have the largest
potential for hydrocarbon energy development in the world, with the
estimated reserves for Mexico alone believed nearly to equal those
in Saudi Arabia.

Ironically, while Latin America has grown in significance
during recent years, the United States has substantially reduced
its official involvement and presence in a number of dimensions.
Direct development aid from the United States fell from $1.1 billion
in 1974 to about $259 million in 1979, with similar levels projected
for the coming years. In the area of cultural and education exchange, despite the high prestige of U.S. universities in Latin
America, there has been a sharp decline from the already modest
level of 1,470 U.S.-sponsored visitors in 1968 to 521 in 1977.
This compares with the Soviet-bloc program, which in 1978 provided
educational grants to 4,659 Latin American students in addition to

55

paying for shorter visits by hundreds, perhaps thousands, of leaders from all sectors.[1]

Military assistance dropped from $142 million in 1976 to $30 million in 1979, while training programs for Latin American officers average $7 million annually. This reduction in bilateral economic aid has been partly offset by U.S. contributions to the World Bank and the Inter-American Development Bank, which have expanded their programs substantially even to the "middle-income" nations (those with more than $1,000 per capita GNP such as Brazil and Mexico) that have recently been defined as ineligible for most bilateral aid.

With these facts in mind, it now becomes possible to focus on the issue of the U.S. national interest. In broad terms, it is in the U.S. national interest that the governments of Latin America be friendly, moderate, and independent of hostile foreign control. Consequently, the most favorable conditions for the United States would exist if each of the Latin American countries were governed by stable democratic regimes that promoted both economic development and social justice. This is demonstrated not only by the consistently good relationships among the democratic nations of the world during this century and by the genuine "security community" that has evolved among democratic Europe, Japan, and North America, but also by the cordial relations the United States has had with virtually all the democratic regimes of Latin America.

The most urgent, specific present danger to the security of the United States is the effort by totalitarian left factions, encouraged and supplied by Cuba and the Soviet Union, to take advantage of Latin America's social and economic problems to gain power wherever they can. In recent years, the United States has failed to take enough of the needed positive and preventive actions, and our government has even been unwilling to provide realistic information about the political purposes and terrorist actions of the extreme left in Central America. This enormous failure of political will and prudence has resulted in the establishment of governments in Grenada and Nicaragua that are now nearly under complete Marxist-Leninist control. It has also permitted Cuban-supported terrorist groups to bring El Salvador to the brink of a Communist takeover; and there has been passivity as the predicted increase in Communist guerilla activity in Guatemala occurred month by month during 1980.

Victory for the extreme left in El Salvador would further polarize Guatemala and probably lead to a tragic increase in violence by its extreme right and left during 1981, with the possibility of Communist victory in 1982. In turn, this would greatly increase the probability that Communist and radical left groups in Mexico, Honduras, and perhaps Panama, with clandestine help from the revolutionary movements in Cuba and Central America, would begin a campaign of destabilization through political action and terror.

Whatever the ultimate outcome, the consequences of major revolutionary violence and the counter-violence likely from the threatened governments (especially Mexico) would include immense human suffering, severe economic dislocations including possible interruptions in Mexican oil production and in the Panama Canal, and large numbers of Mexican refugees who, seeking safety in the United States, would swell the current tide of illegal immigration by several millions if the violence approached the proportions experienced in El Salvador during 1980 (about 9,000 deaths in a population of 4.7 million). There would be billions of dollars in direct economic and social costs for the United States merely to cope with the results of this revolutionary destabilization process whether the extreme left gained power or not.

There would be other large negative results. The continued expansion of revolutionary warfare in the Central America-Mexico region would distract, divide, and demoralize many in the United States, thereby making it less effective in other arenas of American leadership and importance, such as Europe and the Persian Gulf. For most citizens the prospect of an extreme leftist government in Mexico, whatever the deception used and despite initial pledges of "friendly relations," would appear to be a vital threat to the security of American territory as well as an enormous geopolitical setback. Since power is "the capacity to achieve intended effects," the inability of the United States to prevent a successful political war on its doorstep would reduce the confidence of allies and others (such as Persian Gulf regimes) looking to the United States for protection.

Furthermore, the U.S. interest in preventing both the success of Communist revolution in Central America and Mexico and the establishment of any additional Communist regimes in Latin America is also a major defense interest. Cuba has demonstrated the enormous costs of coping with Soviet military installations close to the United States as well as the destructive effects of its Soviet-supplied and encouraged political and military activities in Africa (Angola, Mozambique, Ethiopia), the Persian Gulf (South Yemen), as well as Latin America (support for terrorism in Central America, Colombia, Venezuela, Peru). The failure of the Eisenhower administration to distinguish between democratic and Marxist-Leninist opposition to the Batista dictatorship permitted the consolidation of Communist power in Cuba from 1959 to 1961 and then brought the most severe threat of World War III when the U.S.S.R. attempted to install ballistic missiles in 1962.

At the same time, the success of the existing democratic constitutional governments and those in transition is of major importance to the United States because it provides positive examples for a world order favorable to the democratic nations. The strictly economic aspects of U.S. relationships with Latin America are also important for both partners. Our discussion of Mexico and Brazil will illustrate that prudent and helpful U.S. economic policies

can also have beneficial consequences for our security and world
order interests by providing timely help to prevent severe internal
problems.

II SIGNIFICANT TRENDS AND U.S. POLICY

Given the realities of contemporary Latin America and a prudent regard for our national interests, there are three essential tasks of
a balanced and effective U.S. policy: (A) encourage and support
existing democratic governments and the process of peaceful transition to genuine democracy; (B) prevent extremist and leftist
terrorist groups and their front organizations from taking power;
(C) provide help for successful adaptation to global economic pressures as a way of promoting continued economic growth and better
living conditions.

These three goals are mutually reinforcing if the United States
acts with foresight, prudence, and consistency. Some observers,
usually liberals, make the intellectual mistake of believing that
any change is better than right-wing dictatorship; they fail to
closely examine the political goals, character, and consequences of
Communist and extreme leftist groups. Others, usually conservatives,
fail to understand that social reform and democratic political development are not only intrinsically in the U.S. interest, but that
these ultimately provide the best defense against Communist success.
Often those with a great deal of past experience with the failure
of well-intentioned but poorly thought-out and badly implemented
U.S. policies tend to think that the U.S. government is too incom-
petent and faction-ridden to do anything on behalf of the first two
goals. This discussion departs from all these views and will suggest practical approaches to achieving each of these purposes.

(A) Encouragement for democratic political development

A good definition of democracy is given in Raymond Gastil's Freedom
in the World, 1978 (p. 115):

> There is democracy where rulers are politically respon-
> sible to their subjects. And there is political respon-
> sibility where two conditions hold: where citizens are
> free to criticize their rulers and to come together to
> make demands on them and to win support for the policies
> they favour and the beliefs they hold; and where the
> supreme makers of law and policy are elected to their
> offices at free and periodic elections.

Despite the large amount of conceptual and empirical writing on political development in the last two decades, nearly all this academic
effort has focused on the "structures and functions" of evolving

political systems. Although the work of Easton, Almond, Verba, Huntington, and others has been useful in providing a general frame- work for comparing changes in the organizational style of govern- ments, it has not been concerned with the most difficult task of political development -- the creation of functioning democratic governments accountable to their citizens. Ernst Halperin notes that nearly all academic writing on Latin America during the last decade has followed this "structure functionalist tendency," and the result is that "(we) Latin Americanists have been caught with our pants down. Human rights and democracy are the big issues and we do not know how to fit them into our functionalist model of the political system."[2]

Two premises are fundamental to our consideration of policy. First, political democracy can be attained and lost by societies, and there are means of assessing movement in either direction. Second, there is a distinction between the authoritarian and totali- tarian types of dictatorship, and the prospects for liberalization are far greater in authoritarian regimes. In authoritarian regimes, a large variety of intermediate institutions, such as voluntary associations, labor and business organizations, civic and religious groups, and some partially free media, continue to exist with some degree of independence from the state. In totalitarian dictator- ships, the regime either destroys or dominates these institutions while making far greater effort to obtain positive expressions of ideological loyalty from the population.

The recent return to democratic government in Latin America includes the Dominican Republic (1977), Ecuador (1979), Peru, which ended 12 years of leftist military rule in 1980, and Honduras, where the military government conducted fair elections in April 1980 as a first step back toward constitutional government.

These transitions back to democracy took place at the initia- tive of the leaders and major institutions within these nations. They followed the successful examples set by Spain (1977) and Por- tugal (1976), where more than four decades of dictatorship by the right were followed by the successful restoration of democratic institutions, which required the defeat of the attempt by the Portu- guese Communist Party to seize power in 1975. The European democ- racies along with the United States helped support the democratic political, labor, business, and civic leaders and institutions in Portugal and Spain.

There was, however, no effort to use economic or other pres- sures to tell those countries how or how quickly their existing political systems should be liberalized. In that same spirit, a new U.S. administration could encourage and nurture the forces of political moderation and democracy in Latin America through a variety of open relationships. This is especially important in the fragile recent democracies as well as in countries (such as Brazil, Uruguay, Argentina, and Chile) where the current military governments have embarked on a defined program of liberalization.

In essence, U.S. policy must find the middle ground between the unrealistic interventionism of a crusade and merely routine diplomatic relations in all situations short of visible crisis. There is a domain of useful government and private action where the United States can support democratic forces and weaken those seeking to polarize the hemisphere into either Communist or authoritarian regimes.

A first step in doing this is to transcend the artificial and self-limiting categorization of all policy as either "noninterventionist" or "interventionist." The overall posture of the United States in the region might have several facets. One is normal diplomatic relations dealing with day-to-day interests and bilateral issues with continuity and predictability. High-profile efforts to bring about internal political change using trade, investment credits, aid cutoffs, and the like would occur only in extreme cases. There should, however, be a second level of thought and action concerned with developing practical country-specific strategies for identifying and supporting genuinely democratic groups. This would involve the use of discretionary resources, such as information, communications, and cultural exchange programs, to nurture democratic groups systematically.

One specific example of this type of support is the work of the American Institute for Free Labor Development. This private organization with backing from American labor and business has worked for years in some Latin American countries to help the genuinely democratic trade union, community, and peasant organizations become more effective and compete with the Communist-dominated unions and mass action organizations.* In the last two decades, more than 360,000 democratic labor leaders have been trained, but in recent years the level of government support has in no way matched the need and opportunity for this type of democratic political action.

A third level of effort might be focused on specific countries of interest, either because the pace of transition toward democracy was speeding up, or because the dangers of polarization by extremists were increasing. This could involve the establishment of a semiautonomous organization, which could act separately from the official diplomatic presence; German political foundations such as the Friedrich Ebert Stiftung and the Konrad Adenauer Stiftung are

---

*The tragic deaths on Jan. 4, 1981 of Mr. Michael Hammer, Mr. Mark Pearlman of AIFLD, and Mr. Rodolfo Viera, leader of the agrarian reform program in El Salvador, testified to the personal courage required, because individuals doing this work are often the target of violence by the extreme right or extreme left.

possible models. Among the functions that could be performed at comparatively modest costs by such an entity or by the existing foreign policy institutions are:

actions to increase the sense of solidarity among the existing democratic governments in Latin America, enabling them to establish cooperative links with people and institutions seeking greater democracy;

building of links between newly legalized political parties, trade unions, voluntary associations, and their democratic counterparts in Latin American nations, especially with individuals who have recently made a successful transition;

the encouragement of democratic opposition groups through publication and distribution of their writings and invitations to travel in the democracies;

active engagement in the competition of political ideas by communicating the facts of successful social and economic performance in the democracies, and the repression, poverty, corruption, and elite privilege of Communist regimes such as Cuba; and by using films, media, and books for key audiences;

providing appropriate, accurate information to leaders of democratic groups when extremists make efforts to penetrate and obtain control;

providing advisory help in the conduct of fair elections, monitoring services, and in the establishment of independent parties and media;

reaching out to students and workers from Latin American countries while they are temporarily studying or residing in the United States.

These types of actions would be public, consensual, and directed toward long-term effects. More difficult decisions would need to be made if the United States were to consider moving toward more immediate and direct involvement in particular countries where timely action was essential. A fourth type of policy might involve special political and economic help for threatened, fragile democracies along with direct help to counteract externally supported destabilizing forces. This level of involvement might occur in the context of threatened movement toward the extreme left, as in Nicaragua and El Salvador.

These efforts to support democratic groups in particular countries could also benefit by cooperation with third parties, such as other democratic Latin American or European countries, trade union federations, democratic political parties, and the international links among them, like those among the Social Democratic and the Christian Democratic parties.

(B) Preventing the success of Communist and extreme leftist revolutionary movements

There are three essential realities that seem to have been for-gotten by many concerned with events in Latin America. First, the Soviet bloc, including Cuba, has always defined both peaceful co-existence and detente to include the continuation of the "struggle between the two world systems" by all means short of open military attack. During the last 35 years -- despite the misinformed con-temporary illusions about earlier American supremacy -- the Soviet Union and those it controls have achieved a number of major gains through political warfare (Eastern Europe, China, Southeast Asia, Cuba, and since 1975, Angola, Mozambique, Ethiopia, South Yemen, and Afghanistan). This political warfare is different in each situation, but it employs a blend of propaganda, deception, compe-tent organization, terrorism, and paramilitary methods. Our govern-ment has had great difficulty in taking prudent and timely preven-tive action because these techniques -- often applied through proxies -- intentionally keep the threat ambiguous.

Second, in a particular geographic region, and to some degree in the world, each successive victory of the revolutionary left adds to its power, appeal, and momentum in the next target coun-tries. Third, in foreign affairs, the test of prudence and com-petence is acting in a timely way so that negative trends can be reversed with a minimum of human cost and geopolitical risk (halt-ing the remilitarization of the Rhineland by Nazi Germany in 1936, for example).

In Latin America, the immediate danger is that if the Commu-nist forces consolidate their power in Nicaragua and take El Sal-vador, then 90 million people living from Panama to the U.S. border could be swept unwillingly into Cuban-type totalitarian regimes. Fortunately, from the point of view of the Soviet Union, this pro-cess, while desirable as a means of further weakening its principal adversary, is not worth a major effort in clandestine or public action, and therefore the United States and friendly governments can act with comparatively little risk at present. Nevertheless, this requires a factual understanding of what is really happening in the Central America-Mexico region.

In Nicaragua, two very different political groups joined to-gether to overthrow Somoza in July 1979: the Communist guerrillas and activists who had been receiving Cuban aid since 1962, and a variety of genuinely democratic parties and business and labor groups.

Fidel Castro had won his revolution with a similar coalition, and
in 1961, having eliminated all the Social Democrats and other moderates, he wrote candidly that he had promised free elections and
democratic reform because he did not want his movement to be "very
small and limited...If it had a more radical program...the revolutionary movement against Batista would not of course have gained
the breath...and made possible the victory."[3] Castro also described
how he established an inner power center and kept the moderates
involved in the Council of State and other powerless units until
he could dispose of the "bourgeois remnants."

Despite Castro's candid boasting about his deception of the
moderates inside and outside Cuba, most of the influential U.S.
media and other observers of Latin America have not wanted to make
the definitive operational distinction between the Communist and
the democratic elements of the new Nicaraguan government, nor to
seek ways to limit Cuban-Soviet support to the former and increase
the competitive prospects of the latter.

President Carter failed to act effectively to help the democratic forces, despite knowledge of both the massive Cuban supply
of weapons for the final offensive during June-July 1979 and the
Cuban secret agents who provided the extra resources that could
assure dominance by the Marxist-Leninist groups irrespective of
the hopes of the Nicaraguan people.

Nicaragua has received more than $650 million in economic aid
from the democracies and international lending institutions. None
of this has been translated into effective incentives for democracy.
Elections were postponed until 1985, and they "will serve to reinforce and improve the revolution."[4] The media is under virtually
complete control except for La Prensa. The revolution is continuing
pressure against all non-Sandinista parties and unions, and in
November 1980 an unarmed leader of the business federation was
killed by the police -- perhaps as a warning. In late August
1980, the four democratic parties called upon the OAS and democratic governments to hold the FSLN to its pre-victory written
promise of free elections -- not one word of this poignant appeal
was carried by any of the U.S. prestige media.[5] In foreign policy,
Nicaragua has given clandestine support for the revolutionary
terrorists in El Salvador, it has signed a friendship agreement
with the U.S.S.R., and it has taken a pro-Soviet/Cuban position on
nearly all issues in the United Nations. In a visit to North
Korea, Thomas Borge, the Communist minister of the interior, said:
"The Nicaraguan revolution will not be content until the imperial-
ists have been overthrown in all parts of the world."[6]

At present, real power is in the hands of the nine-person
Directorate chosen in Cuba in consultation with Fidel Castro in
March 1979. It controls the new secret police, the new Army, and the
Sandinista Defense Committees, a neighborhood informant network --
three instruments of social control being established with extensive

Cuban help. Genuinely democratic groups still exist and there is still some chance to prevent a Cuban-style totalitarian state from being consolidated -- but only if much more help (a la Portugal) is given to the democratic forces and if the extreme left fails to win in El Salvador.

In El Salvador three forces are fighting: a reformist coalition, the extreme right, and the extreme left. In March 1980 the reformist coalition enacted a major agrarian reform that provided land for 2.1 million peasants. It has also prevented -- with U.S. help -- two right-wing coups and still can succeed if given more political, economic, intelligence, and military help to support the moderate coalition against the extreme left and right. The centrist coalition consists of the Christian Democrats, most of the military, many democratic unions, and the 160,000-member UCS peasant organization, along with most of the Catholic Church and significant elements of the business community. The extreme right is using some elements of the security forces and various private paramilitary groups to murder moderates as well as members of the extreme left. Its actions have become more destructive as the power of the extreme left has grown; the Christian Democratic leadership has had far more people murdered than the extreme left.

In January 1980, three leftist terrorist organizations, the Communist Party of El Salvador and the two mass action groups (BPR, FPL) formed a united front group now called the Revolutionary Democratic Front (FDR). Since then a consistent political-military strategy aimed at victory in the winter of 1980-81 has been followed: relentless attack on the current government to fragment and isolate it internally, and the international use of propaganda to hold it "responsible for all the violence," along with a steady buildup in the military and organizational strength of the FDR. In 1978 there were an estimated 400 extreme left terrorists; by 1979, about 1,000; and by December 1980, roughly 5,000 facing an army of 12,000 and about 6,000 in paramilitary forces. At the end of December 1980, the members of the Communist government in exile for El Salvador located in Mexico announced they would begin a final military offensive so that Mr. Reagan would "find an irreversible situation in El Salvador by the time he reaches the presidency."[7] As in Nicaragua, the power structure clearly places the completely Marxist-Leninist Unified Revolutionary Directorate (DRU) above the political arm of the FDR. The brutality of the extreme left is best illustrated by their own claims that they accounted for about 5,000 of the estimated 9,000 political deaths during 1980.

(a) The pattern of left revolutionary action and suggestions
     for a balanced approach

There is definitive evidence that since 1978 Cuba has provided important new political, economic, and military support to the left terrorist groups in Central America. Castro has urged unity, prudence, and above all, deception of the United States, to prevent direct or indirect intervention before the revolutionary gains could be made irreversible.

Speaking specifically about Cuban support for the totalitarian left in El Salvador and Guatemala, the administration told the Congress in March 1980 that it includes "advice, propaganda, safe haven, training, arms" (Department of State), "men and material which transit Honduras, (and) aircraft landings at remote haciendas" with weapons from Cuba for the terrorists (Department of Defense).

Internationally, the extreme left has been successful in partially co-opting both Mexico and the democratic Socialist International, especially the German Social Democratic Party and its political foundation -- the Friedrich Ebert Stiftung. In late March 1980, the Socialist International condemned U.S. support for the reformist El Salvador government; in April 1980, the democratic Socialists of El Salvador, with help and encouragement from the SI and the German SPD, joined the "Revolutionary Democratic Front" to work under the leadership of the Communist left as "one more soldier in the revolutionary process." This provides the aura of legitimacy and moderation that the extreme left is using to prevent many U.S. allies in Europe and Latin America from supporting the current government of El Salvador. In December 1980, the temporary suspension of U.S. aid greatly contributed to the isolation of the current government.

A comprehensive and balanced approach in El Salvador requires that the United States provide more political and economic support for peaceful reform while at the same time taking vigorous action against the extreme left terrorist networks and their Cuban support structures, as well as seeking ways to contain and neutralize the extreme right.

The critical judgment to be made is whether there is a better chance of helping the moderate Christian Democratic and military leaders against both extremes by withholding or providing economic or military aid. The withholding strategy has been tried for months (helicopters, military aid) and has clearly failed. The coming weeks probably represent the last chance for the United States to try a supportive strategy that provides the moderates with the economic and military assets they can use to continue the reforms, defeat the extreme left, and neutralize the power of the extreme right. A new policy must include additional communications efforts to affirm democratic values and to tell the truth about life under communism; and it must include intensified economic sanctions against Cuba as long as Castro continues to supply weapons and training for political violence. These approaches could throw the revolutionary left off balance and provide more time to strengthen the moderates in the region.

(b) Central America and relations between the United States
and Mexico

There are three distinguishable aspects to the current U.S.-Mexican
relationship: the Communist threat in Central America and the correct response; the array of normal bilateral relations, including
trade, energy, illegal immigration, air routes/tourism, and water
sharing; and the political climate of the relationship as a result
of views of the elite, influential publics within both nations.

A new administration in Washington can make progress on the
last two issues by competent diplomacy and increased efforts to open
a dialogue with the mostly anti-American opinion-making elites. A
recent public opinion survey found that 70 percent of the Mexican
public was favorable to the United States, but 75 percent believed
the United States was not fair in its economic relations. The
first issue, however, is the most important, the least understood,
and has the most immediate political consequences.

Currently, the Mexican strategy is to support the "leftist coalitions" in Nicaragua, El Salvador, and Guatemala without seeking
or urging any guarantee of free elections, political liberties, or
the like. The Mexican hypothesis is that given the failure of the
Carter administration to halt the Sandinista victory in Nicaragua
in 1979 and the growth of the revolutionary forces in El Salvador
and Guatemala through 1980, its only successful strategy must be
to "moderate the extremist left by supporting the revolutionary
groups."[8]

Examples of this discreet but officially sanctioned support
include: Nicaragua -- breaking relations with Somoza (May 1979),
permitting Cuban and Sandinista support elements to be based in
Mexico, and facilitating the flow of money and cadres through
Mexico in 1979; El Salvador -- during 1980, consistently supporting the revolutionary groups in El Salvador (the Mexican government
party, the PRI, acting for the government, gave permission for the
Revolutionary Democratic Front [FDR] government in exile to use
Mexican territory), facilitating aid shipments, extensively supporting, through the PRI apparatus (funds, propaganda, safe
houses), action against any Honduran support for the El Salvador
government, and holding a Conference of World Solidarity with
the revolution in El Salvador in November; further, the government-
linked trade unions (CTM) called for the termination of diplomatic
relations and suspension of oil sales; Guatemala -- during 1980,
official distancing from the current government, combined with
tacit acquiescence in the establishment in Mexico of arms supply
networks, small training areas, and medical facilities for the
Communist guerrillas in Guatemala.

The United States must communicate to Mexico that it under-
stands the Mexican strategy but believes it is mistaken because
of the fundamental differences in outlook and power between the

hard-core Communist groups that control the "leftist coalition" in Nicaragua, El Salvador, and Guatemala, and the moderate, reformist left that Mexico hopes to encourage. The United States has definitive evidence that the leadership of the Central American revolutionary groups is Communist and firmly tied to Cuba and the U.S.S.R.

A better way to promote reform, stability, and constitutional government would be an approach that consists of support for the center, as well as democratic left forces, and that condemns equally the violence of the extreme left and extreme right. Mexico is a sovereign state and of course will pursue its own policy. However, it would be advisable to discuss the fact and alternatives at greater length in the very near future. Since a revolutionary Guatemala might become a sanctuary for guerrillas and terrorists operating in the southern, oil-rich regions of Mexico, the consequence of being wrong about strategy could be very severe.

(C) Assistance for adaptation to global economic pressures -- the example of Brazil

The prospects for improved living conditions, political liberalization, and stability in Latin America will be greater during this decade if the economic growth rates of the last 30 years are continued. Latin American economies on the whole performed well after the 1973 OPEC oil-price increase as a result of structural changes and because of a massive increase in public and private loans from the industrial democracies. The World Bank's reports indicate that the foreign debt increased from $22 billion in 1970 to $140 billion by the beginning of 1980. The combination of continued OPEC price increases, the large foreign debt service payments, a reduction in export growth due to economic slowdowns in OECD nations, and the unwillingness of oil-exporting nations to make their capital surpluses directly available to the developing countries are creating a mounting economic crisis.

Among the nations of the world, Brazil ranks 7th in population (120 million), 10th in GNP ($213 billion in 1980), and covers nearly half the vast South American continent. It is the world's 4th largest agricultural exporter, and among oil-importing developing countries, Brazil has the largest value of exports. Brazil has immense strategic importance for and influence on the destiny of Latin America. Continuous economic and political stability and progress would have a positive effect in the region, while a growing economic crisis and political polarization might have very destructive consequences. The industrial democracies currently have a $72 billion stake in its economic performance, including $23 billion in U.S. loans ($16 billion) and investments ($7 billion).

Brazil illustrates the severity of the economic problems and the requirement for U.S. participation and perhaps leadership

in a multinational effort to work out new public-private financing
methods to prevent sharp economic contractions.

The private leaders have a tendency to downplay the seriousness of such potential problems because they do not want to risk a
disinvestment stampede that becomes a self-fulfilling prophecy.
The IMF and World Bank (total annual lending $15 billion) alone do
not possess adequate resources. There is also a need for action
in advance of a visible crisis, which in Brazil could be accompanied
by threats from either the right or left extremes (more likely the
right) and could halt the liberalization process and risk severe
social conflict, which would in turn reduce the prospects for financial help from abroad. The outlines of a sensible program would
include efforts to use OPEC capital surpluses, along with OECD
government funds and guarantees, to refinance the current debt in
return for internal economic policies that are responsible, job
creating, and redistributive or least harmful to the poor.

III LATIN AMERICA IN THE GLOBAL CONTEXT OF U.S. FOREIGN POLICY

Under the current historical circumstances, U.S. foreign policy
must be effective in a number of concurrently vital tasks, which
include: maintaining adequate military forces; strengthening the
alliance bonds with Europe and Japan; preventing additional radical or pro-Soviet regimes from coming to power in the Persian Gulf
regions; and, preventing the establishment of additional Communist
regimes in this hemisphere, most importantly, preventing any major
revolutionary violence or destabilization in Mexico. Each of these
is interrelated. The essential alliance among the democracies can
be threatened by military weakness that leads to allied appeasement,
or by additional Libyan-type regimes gaining control of the oil
supply for Europe and Japan, an event that would certainly link oil
sales to economic and political conditions -- most likely related
to Israel -- and that would be intended to separate the United
States from its more oil-dependent allies.

Consider the damaging effect on the credibility of the United
States with its allies, or in the Middle East context, of a several-
year process of revolutionary violence in Mexico with casualties
proportionate to those in El Salvador (i.e., 126,000 deaths), or an
"Iran-like" anti-American, radical, faction-ridden government, or,
in the worst case, a pro-Soviet Communist regime in Mexico. The
Palestinian terrorist groups have supplied extensive financial,
training, and weapons support to the extreme left in Central America,
because they understand this essential geopolitical connection.[9]
The PLO opened its Brazilian mission in 1972, its Mexican office in
1975, and its "embassy" in Nicaragua in 1980, where Arafat stated
that "the triumph of the Nicaraguans is the PLO's triumph." The
extreme left in El Salvador provides a foretaste of the foreign
policy it will follow by consistently condemning the "ultrarightist
alliance of Washington, Tel Aviv, Guatemala City and Caracas."[10]

In essence, Moscow, Havana, the PLO, and other adversaries of the United States recognize that should several left extremist governments take power in Central America it will weaken Washington everywhere. As with the change of regime in Iran, few U.S. allies are concerned at present because they do not believe this could really happen. The negative political consequences will be <u>clearly</u> visible only after the formation of a pro-Cuban bloc in Central America. Only then will the leaders in Europe and the Middle East and Asia recognize fully the magnitude of the negative impact on the U.S. capacity for action in their regions.

Would a more balanced U.S. policy in Latin America bring about conflict with other allies or interests? The most serious difficulty might arise with the Social Democratic Parties of Europe, especially Germany, because of the gradual but very dramatic change in the Socialist International, a confederation of the major <u>democratic</u> Socialist Parties of the world. The Socialist International originally had been distinct from the Communist International because of its commitment to democracy and individual political rights. Unfortunately, these basic values have been obscured in more and more cases by a loosely defined ideology of Third World empathy, which, for example, defines the PLO as the "only legitimate representative of the Palestinian people" and sanctions terrorism against anything called "imperialism" or "reaction."

In Central America the German government, the German Social Democratic Party, and the Socialist International are in effect supporting the terrorist left. In 1980, citing security concerns, Germany closed its embassy in El Salvador and suspended its economic aid program.[11] The German SPD political foundation has wide-ranging contacts among the democratic left in all of Latin America. Washington had been hoping that the German Social Democrats would use their enormous influence and financial resources to urge a coalition of all democratic groups against the extreme left and extreme right just as they did in 1975 to rescue Portugal from what Kissinger believed was an unstoppable Communist takeover. In March 1980, the State Department sent a senior official to brief former Chancellor Willy Brandt on the information that showed the revolutionary left in El Salvador was Communist, tightly linked to Cuba, and also received considerable military and financial help from Palestinian terrorist groups. Nevertheless, at the first meeting of the Socialist International held in Latin America, neither Brandt, as its president, nor the German delegation, protested the meeting's final resolutions, which condemned U.S. policy in El Salvador, rejected the agrarian reforms as a false "program of 'reforms and repressions'," and warned against "North American military intervention." At the same time, this meeting of democratic Socialists invited Fidel Castro to speak as an honored guest, voted unanimously that independence rather than self-determination was the "only solution" for Puerto Rico, and urged an alliance with the Communist left in Central America.[12]

In June 1980 the Socialist International stated that it "fully
supports the struggle of the FDR...in El Salvador." In late July
a key adviser to Chancellor Schmidt came to Washington and learned
in detail how much financial and political support Germany and the
SPD had been giving the extreme left in Central America. He promised
to make an independent inquiry, to halt some planned actions intended
to give more help to the violent left, to try to get the embassy
reopened, and to restore economic aid. So far, few of these positive
steps have occurred in connection with that visit. The prestigious
Frankfurter Allgemeine Zeitung (July 23, 1980) raised this question:
How can Germany expect American support against the Soviet Union if
it is active on "the side of a violent left joined in a popular
front as vassals of Cuban-indoctrinated communists?" Despite evidence that the agrarian reform in El Salvador had benefited hundreds of thousands of peasants, the November 1980 meeting of the
Socialist International again failed to condemn both the extreme
left and extreme right in Central America.

Several factors explain this important difference in perspective. Many Social Democrats from Central America have simply given
up hope for reform and have decided that violent revolution is the
only way to overcome the brutality of the extreme right. They do
not want to know about the fate of thousands of moderates in other
nations who have preceded them into the oblivion of important coalition with effective, disciplined, and externally supported Communist groups. These misguided Social Democrats have in turn found
ready support among the more leftist elements in the German Social
Democratic Party -- the 30 percent of its activists who in 1979
professed to see no problem with the Soviet invasion of Afghanistan,
and who think of the Soviet Union as a "transitional society with
some authoritarian features" rather than as a mature totalitarian
state.

The wishful thinking about Nicaragua that ignores the evidence of growing Marxist dominance, and the Mexican strategy of
seeking to moderate the revolutionary movements by joining them
have combined together into a collage of illusions that has neither
been explicitly accepted nor rejected by the Social Democratic
leadership of Europe. Instead, they consider Latin America of
primary interest to the United States. Their failure to be more
informative and persuasive has permitted their policy toward the
Central American revolutions to remain on a collision course with
Washington.

Nevertheless, it is likely that a new administration could, with
greater effort, be able to convince the moderate majorities in the
leading Democratic Socialist Parties in Europe and most of Latin
America that their support should be given only to genuinely democratic groups not associated with the Communist or violent left.
Moreover, if there is no change in German and Socialist International
policies in the near future, and if Central America does become Communist, there are likely to be severe recriminations when the

American political leadership and public come to understand the
destructive role played by their ostensible allies, especially the
Federal Republic of Germany.

Conclusion

Ultimately, different concepts of history underline much of the debate about desirable U.S. foreign policies. There is a strong intellectual current, actually a very traditionalist view, that large
impersonal "forces" determine the destiny of nations and governments. For some, like the Marxists, who believe they are riding
the tide of history, the policy corollary is activism. For others,
who have no simple dogmas of historical inevitability, it is often
a wishful or merely detached passivity. A recent article illustrated this latter policy viewpoint in its reference to a list of
"floundering" governments, including El Salvador, Guatemala,
Saudi Arabia, Kuwait, Egypt, Indonesia, and South Korea: "The
best course for Ronald Reagan may be to let history sweep (them)
away." This advice also assumed that any U.S. attempt to shape
the future would lead to a "waste of dollars in volatile, less-
important countries just to try to exercise control."[13]

Quite clearly this discussion has proceeded from a rather different perspective, which assumes that history is the cumulative
result of conscious decisions by individuals, groups, and societies
motivated by ideas, visions, interests, fears, and hopes---often in
ambiguous juxtaposition. Democratic political change is accomplished by committed people or groups, and it should be the task of
a great democracy like the United States to nurture and encourage
these individuals by a variety of positive, open, and consensual
means. In the same way, Communist revolution is the product of
action by individuals and groups, often highly disciplined and
motivated to create a "better society" as they define it. It is
possible and it is necessary for the United States to prevent
further Communist success in this hemisphere. Postponing this
task will make the human costs greater and the risks to peace more
severe as first Cuba and then the Soviet Union invest their prestige
and their power in the maintenance of any new Communist regime
that consolidates their power.

Timely action will prevent more millions of people from enduring the agony of another repressive Communist political economy.
The Vietnam argument against containment in this hemisphere is
misleading because the strategic equation is reversed -- there,
the U.S.S.R., China, and North Vietnam could funnel enormous military resources into a war of attrition without concern for casualties. In the Western Hemisphere, there is not yet any reason to
use U.S. combat forces. All the elements of strategic advantage,
intellectual and material, rest with the United States.

Properly understood and implemented, the three elements of
U.S. policy for Latin America are mutually reinforcing -- preventing the spread or success of revolutionary violence and terror
is a corollary of democratic political development. And, both purposes will be served by timely help to maintain economic growth.

The recent failure of prudent foresight in the Middle East
explains why the United States now expects to spend $20-$30 billion
for a Rapid Deployment Force of 110,000 men, which may have limited
utility in any major Persian Gulf crisis. The current costs of a
prudent and balanced U.S. policy for Latin America are so modest
that they do not compete with the resources needed for any other
region. The requirements for success are realism, good judgment,
cooperative action with Latin America, and the institutional disci-
pline to carry out consistent policies once decisions have been
agreed upon.

NOTES

[1]Data is from the World Bank, but an excellent interpretive analy-
sis of the last three decades is, Joseph R. Ramos, "Dependency and
Development: An Attempt to Clarify the Issues," DOCLA, September-
October 1978, Santiago, Chile.

[2]Ernst Halperin, "The State of Latin American Studies," Washington
Quarterly, Vol. 2, April 1978, pp. 99-111. Among the few analytic
discussions of the process of building and achieving democracy are
Developing Democracy (1972) by William A. Douglas; and Seymour M.
Lipset's Political Man (1959); and the writing of Raymond Gastil.
The Wilson Center program's focus on democratic transitions
is a welcome additional effort in this sparse field.

[3]From Revolucion, December 1961; also quoted in Theodore Draper,
Castroism - Myths and Realities, 1964.

[4]A CIA intelligence report of May 1979, leaked to the press in
late July 1979, demonstrated that the Carter administration had
timely warning and factual information concerning the extent of
Cuban and DGI support for the FSLN Directorate.

[5]FSLN Directorate member quoted by Jeane Kirkpatrick, "U.S. Security and Latin America," Commentary, January 1981.

[6]Foreign Broadcast Information Service (FBIS), August 26, 1980.

[7]New York Times, December 27, 1980, "Salvadoran Rebels Predict Final Offensive."

[8]For an extensive discussion of this see my chapter, "Mexican Foreign Policy," in The Future of Mexico, Hudson Institute, 1980.

[9]For a number of well-documented examples of this support see the testimony of U.S. Representative William Young before the House Foreign Affairs Committee, Inter-American subcommittee, September 30, 1980.

[10]FBIS, May 17, 1980. It has escaped many observers that Israel has been a major declared enemy of the revolutionary left in Central America.

[11]Bradley Graham, "Bonn's Tilt in Central America Causes Worry in Washington," Washington Post, September 1, 1980.

[12]See the article by Rita Freedman, "Mixed Thoughts on Santo Domingo," Socialist Affairs, May 1980, and the resolutions of the Socialist International meetings published there, which in-cluded the astonishing condemnation of the democratic elections in Honduras during April 1980.

[13]Richard Feinberg, "Preserving U.S. Interests in the Third World When Regimes Are Floundering," New York Times, January 5, 1981. One of the best current discussions that illustrates the cumulatively negative impact of movement toward pro-Soviet regimes in the Third World is Cord Meyer's Facing Reality: From World Federalism to the CIA, 1980, especially the discussions of help for the democratic left in Chile and the failure to provide timely help to pro-Western African groups (chapters 9 and 12).

U.S.-LATIN AMERICAN RELATIONS IN THE 1980s

Abraham F. Lowenthal

I Latin America and the United States: Changing Realities

In a recent Wilson Center conference bringing together selected
opinion leaders from Venezuela and the United States, former White
House counsel Theodore C. Sorensen noted that North Americans
feel like protesting: that Venezuelans take U.S. friendship for
granted just because we are in Venezuela's backyard; that Venezuela
pays more attention to its worldwide commitments (e.g., to OPEC)
than to its bilateral relationship with the United States; that
decisions of major consequence to millions of North American fami-
lies are being taken in the boardrooms of Caracas without the participation of or even consultation with anyone from the United
States; that the terms of trade between Venezuela and the United
States are ever more unfavorable to this country -- in short, they
feel like protesting America's dependence.

Perhaps Mr. Sorensen, like the proverbial lady, did protest
too much. But his jocular intervention does serve to highlight
how much the Western Hemisphere has changed during the 20 years
since John F. Kennedy took office in Washington and proclaimed --
unilaterally, of course -- the "Alliance of Progress."

It is worth insisting on this point as the necessary background
for discussing U.S. interests and policies in the Americas.

Twenty years ago, the United States saw itself as a successful
country in almost every sphere, dealing with Latin American and
Caribbean nations that were not similarly blessed.

Ours was a prosperous and growing economy, the strongest in
the world by far and the linchpin of international trade and finance.
Latin America's economies, in turn, were weak. Many (mis)managed
to combine stagnation, high unemployment, and galloping inflation
-- a cruel mix Washington thought avoidable, if not theoretically
impossible.

Ours was an efficient society of hardworking people committed
to achieving results today, not manana, and motivated to do so
because almost everyone was experiencing material improvement in
his or her own situation and expected more of the same. Latin
American workers seemed less disciplined, less satisfied, less
hopeful, and less productive. Those North Americans who traveled
often commented on the disgraceful state of Latin American public
services (transportation, schools, the mail, the telephone), as
if to underline the contrast between North and South.

Ours was a fiscally responsible and prudent system, featuring
balanced budgets from the family to the federal level and empha-
sizing sound investment policies. Chronic deficits and even defaults
were common in Latin America, where people tended to borrow from
tomorrow to spend today. Too little was being invested in Latin
America, and too much destined for social services. Uruguay epitomized the problem with its expensive social security system
growing faster than its productive base.

We in the United States saw ourselves as an harmonious society, increasingly integrated socially and ethnically, committed
fully to equality and opportunity, and even, in time, to equality
of result. Latin America, in contrast, seemed a continent divided
by class, race, and privilege. Tensions in Latin America were
thought to be mounting, so that the region faced either peaceful
reform or violent revolution.

The United States saw itself 20 years ago as a stable,
participatory democracy with effective political institutions,
strong parties, a self-confident presidency, a judiciary beyond
reproach, and a unique system of separate institutions sharing
powers. Latin America, in contrast, was characterized by endemic
political instability fed by low levels of participation and of
civic trust, a high degree of corruption, weak institutions, and
intensifying social demands.

And 20 years ago, the United States was self-confidently
involved across the world, ready -- as Kennedy put it in his in-
augural address -- to "bear any burden" internationally. Our
military force and our economic and political prowess eclipsed
that of every other nation. Latin America, in contrast, was focus-
ing inward its economic development strategy and was actually
reducing its involvement in international affairs. The active role
some Latin American states had played in the United Nations right
after World War II was giving way 20 years ago to a more self-
absorbed concern with economic development.

The world, and the hemisphere, look very different today.

The U.S. economy, having worsened for years, is in obvious
trouble. International comparative advantage is shifting away
from the United States on item after item. This country's share of

world trade is falling (from 23 percent of the world trade in
manufactured goods in 1970 to 16 percent in 1979) even as the
importance of trade for the U.S. economy is increasing (accounting
for 20 percent of the country's GNP in 1979, up from 6.5 percent
in the 1950s). The North American work ethic has deteriorated as
aspirations and expectations have declined. Unemployment is high
-- well over 10 percent in some states, over 20 percent in some
sectors. Inflation is apparently beyond decisive reversal. Capital
is scarce and increasingly expensive, with the prime rate of interest now over 20 percent for the first time ever. Bankruptcies and
defaults are increasingly common, and are predicted to multiply.
Public services are ever more starved, with the result that mail
is delayed, school programs are cut back, telephone circuits are
busy, trains are dropped, and garbage accumulates. The "politics
of scarcity," of scrambling for advantage in a "zero-sum society,"
threatens to replace the "politics of plenty."

Economic downturn has been accompanied by political decline.
No U.S. president since Eisenhower has left office voluntarily.
The prestige of the presidency has dropped with each new failure.
Political institutions of all kinds are in disrepute -- not just
the presidency but the Congress, the parties, even the Supreme
Court. Corruption and scandal have reached new depths, with mem-
bers of Congress and others convicted of crimes ranging from sex-
ual escapades to selling influence to supposed sheiks.

In this troubling context, special interest groups and single-
issue constituencies press their advantage avidly, using all the
techniques available, from direct mail listings and massive, tar-
geted funding to clogging the streets of Washington with tractors.
Overall stalemate often results. The consequent frustration reflects itself sometimes in apathy -- the 1980 presidential elections drew out the smallest percentage of registered voters since
1948 -- or sometimes in riots, like those that shook Miami in
1980. Even a president elected with an overwhelming mandate must
wonder whether his job can be done well.

Economic and political troubles have contributed to and in
turn been exacerbated by many cleavages in North American society:
among black, brown, and white; between new and older immigrants;
between the Northeast and the Southwest; between rural and urban;
between the "moral majority" and the rest of society; between women
and men; between gays and straights; and among rich, middle class,
and poor. Mr. Reagan's impressive victory notwithstanding, discord
plagues the United States today. And some, at least, see a next
stage ahead of "friendly fascism," of a response to "democratic
distempers" that will build social cohesion at the expense of
individual rights.

And when it comes to international affairs, The Wilson Center's
series of seminar discussions serves to remind us how much the United
States has already withdrawn from the hegemonic position it occupied

in 1960. Expelled from Cuba, defeated in Vietnam, thwarted in Angola, humiliated in Iran, the United States looks today like a power in retreat. Appearances are partly deceiving, but they also reflect the real relative decline in the military power, economic strength, and political influence of the United States.

On most of these various dimensions, Latin American realities are much more positive, in turn, than seemed likely 20 years ago. Economically, the region has enjoyed sustained (if uneven) growth averaging over 6 percent per year since 1960, the best record over the entire period of any group of market economies. Productivity and production continue to rise in most of the region, which by now has a palpable weight in the world economy, likely by 1985 to equal that displaced by all of Western Europe in 1970. The structure of most Latin American economies has shifted from traditional dependence on primary products to the production and export of manufactured goods. (More than 27 percent of Brazil's exports in 1976 were manufactured goods, compared with 3 percent in 1960 -- and more than 52 percent of Mexico's, compared with 12 percent in 1960.) Whereas the combined share of the world's economic production accounted for by the United States and Canada fell from 49.4 percent in 1960 to 34.5 percent in 1975 and is still falling, Latin America's total share rose from 6.2 percent to 7.4 percent and is still climbing, an impressive achievement that would be even more striking if oil production were excluded from the statistics. By and large, Latin American countries have managed better than most in the world -- industrialized or less developed -- to adjust to the rising costs of energy and of capital. Serious problems remain, particularly in the small nations where economies of scale are difficult and extreme vulnerability to external conditions persist, and in the larger economies that have mainly used massive foreign debt to fuel growth -- but the overall economic record is unquestionably impressive.

Socially, Latin America's inequities largely persist, as income remains concentrated as much as or in some cases even more than was the case 20 years ago. Whole segments of countries -- the northeast in Brazil, and the highlands in the Andean countries -- still remain depressingly poor, as does all of Haiti, and several of the Caribbean ministates. But there has also been impressive change in much of Latin America. A generation of growth and some experiences with directed change -- Chile's "revolution in liberty," Peru's military-led experiment, Mexico's continuing reforms -- have produced lasting results. On many indicators -- literacy, health, nutrition, housing -- most of Latin America has made substantial progress since 1961, with and then without the Alliance. Discontent and the objective bases of it survive, but Latin Americans share heightened aspirations, reflected in the region's massive urbanization.

Politically, Latin America appears to be emerging, albeit by fits and starts, from its long experience with authoritarian repression. Central America's dynasties are crumbling, as those in the Caribbean did 20 years ago. Democratic political processes and institutions are once again coming to establish their resilience and their worth, at least in some important countries. In Brazil, the region's largest and most powerful nation, the congressional elections of 1978 saw a substantial popular majority register approval of the liberal opposition movement, which now controls almost half the seats in Congress; the move toward political opening continues despite (or perhaps in part because of) significant economic and social pressures. Military governments -- which were ruling in every South American country but Colombia, Venezuela, and Guyana in 1975 -- now are beginning to give way to elected regimes. In Peru, where the armed forces ruled from 1968 to 1980, former President Fernando Belaunde Terry has regained office with massive support, after an election in which all the significant candidates were dedicated opponents of the military regime. Ecuador is even further advanced on a similar course. Argentina seems to be struggling in the same direction.

Internationally, South America's main nations and some of the region's smaller states -- particularly in the Caribbean -- are ever more fully involved in world trade and financial markets and in various international fora.

Brazil, already the world's 10th largest economy and expected to be the 6th largest by 1990, is the World Bank's principal borrower, the world's second largest exporter of iron ore and of agricultural products, and is a generally powerful influence on a wide range of international issues. Mexico, with major oil and gas reserves in addition to a burgeoning industrial sector, is expected to be the world's 12th largest economy by the end of the century. Already Mexico ranks near Brazil as a massive borrower in international money markets; the two together account for over one-fourth of all loans disbursed to developing countries. Venezuela, a founding member of OPEC, continues to occupy a central place in international energy discussions. Argentina, beginning to pull itself out of a long period of national trauma, aspires to play a leading role among the intermediately developed countries. Together or separately, Latin American countries have been active and influential in the Group of 77, the UNCTAD, the negotiations on the law of the seas, and in the "Nonaligned Movement."

All these trends and processes -- economic growth and restructuring, social change, political opening, and international involvement -- are uneven, fragile, and subject to slowdown or even some reversal. One runs the risk of exaggerating both Latin America's emergence and North America's decline in this kind of telegraphic presentation. The risk is worth taking, however, to underline the point: that power is being redistributed in the Western Hemisphere, from North to South.

The United States is still by far the strongest nation of the Americas, measured by any indicator. But the relative influence of the United States is declining. Long gone are the days when the United States was "practically sovereign" in the Western Hemisphere, as Secretary of State Richard Olney once put it. Gone, too, are the more recent days of the Alliance for Progress, when the United States could comfortably define the agenda and the modalities of inter-American discourse.

The decline of U.S. hegemony, and of the bases for America's "hegemonic presumption," can be conclusively documented with a few examples:

Latin America as a whole sent half its exports to the United States in 1950; the figure was 32 percent by 1975;

Latin America took 56 percent of its imports from the United States in 1950; the figure was 25.5 percent in 1977;

In 1965 the United States accounted for over half of Brazil's foreign direct investment; by 1979 the U.S. share was about 3 percent;

The United States supplied almost all of Latin America's weapons from World War II until 1965; by the late 1970s U.S. arms sales in South America were being exceeded by those of Germany, France, Russia, and even Israel and Brazil itself.

U.S. military assistance in the Americas declined to $30 million in 1979, barely 1 percent of the worldwide total;

The United States had about 800 security advisers assigned in Latin America in 1968; fewer than 100 were assigned in 1979;

U.S. government-sponsored international visitors from Latin America fell from 889 in 1968 to 340 in 1977. U.S. government grants to Latin Americans to study in the United States declined from 591 in 1968 to 181 in 1977, compared with Soviet-bloc funding in 1978 for 4,650 Latin Americans to study in Communist institutions;

The U.S.S.R. had embassies in only 3 countries of Latin America and the Caribbean in 1963, in 7 by 1969, and in 17 by 1980; Russian trade with Latin America multiplied 15 times during the 1970s;

In 1965 the United States could get two-thirds of the members of the Organization of American States to vote for the creation of an Inter-American Peace Force to make collective the unilateral U.S. military intervention in the Dominican Republic; a formal U.S. proposal in the OAS in 1979 to create a similar force would have been overwhelmingly rejected had it not been withdrawn;

Mexico's and Brazil's votes for the 1975 U.N. resolution
identifying Zionism as "racism"; Brazil's early recognition of the
Soviet-backed Popular Movement for the Liberation of Angola (MPLA);
Mexico's initiative in promoting the Charter of Economic Rights and
Duties of States and its successful efforts to reduce the percentage
of its necessary oil exports going to the United States; Venezuela's
role in OPEC; Brazil's nuclear arrangement with Germany; Argentina's
defiance of the grain embargo against the Soviet Union; tiny Grenada's OAS vote on Russia's side of the Afghanistan issue; Cuba's
military interventions in Africa -- all illustrate the increased
willingness and capacity of the Latin American and Caribbean nations
to assert themselves, despite Washington's wishes.

I trust my point has been made.

The proper starting point for any discussion of U.S.-Latin
American relations in the 1980s is the realization that the United
States will need positively to engage the interests of Latin
American and Caribbean nations in pursuit of common objectives --
that Washington can no longer expect to ignore Latin America, much
less to line up a compliant set of Latin American and Caribbean
states behind U.S. aims.

II U.S. Interests with respect to Latin America and the Caribbean

The concept of "national interest" obscures about as much as it
clarifies for the reasons articulated by Alexander George and Robert
Keohane in their recent essay, "The Concept of National Interest:
Uses and Limitations."

Still, it is obviously useful to ask whether what happens in
Latin America and the Caribbean makes any difference to the United
States, and if so, how, why, and how much.

My basic argument is simply stated: What happens in Latin
America during the 1980s will mean much less than it used to (or
than many area specialists still assert) on the traditional dimensions in which U.S. interests have been discussed, but the region
has considerable and growing significance in ways that will become
increasingly central to U.S. foreign policy in the 1980s.

Traditional discussions recite a familiar litany of U.S. security, economic, and political interests: guarding against military
threats to this country, or to its supply of vital raw materials;
protecting maritime routes; promoting and protecting U.S. investment; expanding the market of U.S. exports; winning diplomatic
support in various international fora; and simply enhancing
neighborly harmony and regional solidarity. Major orienting concepts underlying historic U.S. policies toward Latin America were
fashioned when the region was the main area of U.S. foreign

investment and accounted for a big share of U.S. trade, when Pan-American cooperation was vital, and when direct military threats to the United States could be imagined in or through Latin America and the Caribbean.

Things have changed. No direct military threat to the United States is likely to be mounted from locations in the Western Hemisphere. Indeed, the most easily imaginable contingencies for the use of U.S. forces in the Western Hemisphere involve not safeguarding vital U.S. security assets, but rather protecting residual and essentially symbolic U.S. enclaves (in the Panama Canal Zone and at Guantanamo Bay) against local irredentist violence. The direct economic significance of Latin America for the United States is declining relative to that of other regions on the traditional dimensions of U.S. investment and exports. (Latin America's share of U.S. foreign investment fell from 38 percent in 1950 to 18 percent in 1977, for example.)

And Latin America's presumed political solidarity with the United States is no longer either as assured or as significant as it used to be, in an era of Latin American assertiveness on the one hand and of "automatic majorities" on the other.

But the ultimate importance for the United States of what happens in Latin America and the Caribbean is increasing, I would argue, for the following reasons:

a) The direct influence of Latin America -- and especially of Brazil, Mexico, Venezuela, and Argentina -- on the world economy is steadily increasing, and the impact of Latin America's economic fate on our own is ever more significant as the country's dependence on its international economic involvements becomes greater and more obvious. If Latin America's economies were to suffer severe decline, the consequences would be felt elsewhere in the world, but particularly in the United States, the source of so much of Latin America's capital, technology, and other imports. Conversely, there is little doubt that Latin America's continuing expansion has helped the United States to deal with the problem of petro-dollar recycling and to expand its exports. Moreover, under the proper conditions, Latin America's exports could make a significant dent on the problem of inflation in the United States.

b) Latin America can potentially play a crucial role in reforming and strengthening international economic rules and procedures to allow for the continued expansion of world trade and the continued free flow of capital and labor, rather than the adoption of neo-mercantilist "beggar thy neighbor" policies, which would ultimately harm the United States. No liberal international economic reform will endure if it fails to win the support and acceptance of the increasingly powerful middle-income countries of the world, many of the most important of which are Latin American.

    c) Latin American nations, especially the larger ones, are well situated to contribute importantly to helping to resolve (or to worsen) some of what will be the central problems in international affairs during the 1980s: how to expand energy and food production and improve their distribution and use; how to use and conserve the resources of the seas (and of land and space) more efficiently and equitably; how to reduce resource depletion and pollution and deal with their consequences; how to curb the diversion of funds to military purposes, especially how to limit the spread of nuclear and other ready weapons; and how to strengthen international institutional capacities for dealing with all these problems. It is fair to say that none of these major global problems can be effectively dealt with absent the active participation of major Latin American nations.

    d) A few Latin American nations -- particularly Mexico and most of the Caribbean islands -- will have a direct effect on the conditions and quality of life in the United States through the massive migration of their citizens to this country. Millions of persons from Mexico and the Caribbean enter the United States each year, pushed by lack of employment opportunities in their own countries and drawn by conditions here. The capacity of Mexico and the Caribbean countries to meet the needs of their own people will affect important aspects of employment, education, social relations, public health, and politics in this country.

    e) Less demonstrably but no less importantly, conditions in Latin America and the Caribbean will affect the ambience and the conditions for the continued expression of basic values at the core of American society. The rise of bureaucratic authoritarian regimes in Latin America in recent years, many of them aided to power directly or indirectly by U.S. policies, has raised troubling questions for North Americans about the continued viability of representative democracy, constitutional government, and the protection of fundamental human rights. It is in the interest of the United States to encourage and show the continued relevance of approaches to development based on individual autonomy, social equality, civic participation, and the respect of basic human rights.

    In sum, Latin American and Caribbean societies will be important for the United States during the 1980s because of their economic and political weight internationally (Brazil, Mexico, and to a lesser extent Argentina and Venezuela will be important on this dimension); because of their degree of interdependence with the United States, economically and demographically (Mexico, the Caribbean countries, and to a lesser extent Brazil and Venezuela will be most important on this dimension); and because of the impact of conditions there -- and of the U.S. role -- on the ambience for preserving fundamental U.S. values (a consideration affecting U.S. relations with the whole region, but especially with the Caribbean and with those countries struggling to preserve or restore constitutional regimes). These U.S. interests -- rather than axiomatic

responses to hegemony lost -- should orient U.S. policies in
the 1980s.

Important likely developments in Latin America and the Caribbean
during the 1980s

Predictions of the future necessarily are based on one's projections
of recent trends as one interprets them, and take too little account
of the contingent, the accidental, and the discontinuous. Moreover,
what happens in a region like Latin America will surely be shaped in
some measure by what happens elsewhere in the world, including in
part by the way in which the United States deals with the area. It
is misleading to think of the United States as if it were an actor
outside the international system, waiting for developments elsewhere in the world in order to determine its own policies.

These caveats having been stated, let me cooperate with the
seminar's organizers by listing 10 developments I think likely
during the 1980s, and important for the United States.

1) Led by Brazil, Mexico, Argentina, and Colombia, Latin
America's economies will continue their dynamism during the 1980s,
and will base much of their growth on the export of manufactured
products. They will press to increase their share of the market in
the United States and in other industrial countries, and will compete effectively with the industrialized countries in Third World
markets.

2) Led by Brazil, Mexico, Peru, and Venezuela, the Latin
American economies will continue to be major claimants on capital
from other parts of the world. Their reliance on debt -- from
international financial institutions and from the commercial bank-
ing systems -- will pose major challenges to international monetary and financial systems.

3) Brazil will continue its emergence as a major economic and
political influence. It will present the United States with a
number of challenges: access to our markets, capital, and technology; pressure for cooperation in dealing with its expanding need
for energy; and competition for influence and advantage in other
regions. The United States will have more conflict in the 1980s
with capitalist Brazil than with Communist China.

4) Mexico will accelerate its emergence as a significant industrial power and as a major producer and exporter of oil and gas.
Both cooperation and conflict betwen the United States and Mexico
are likely to increase during the 1980s, in an increasingly complex
and important relationship. Conflicts will take place on many
issues, such as access to U.S. markets for manufacturers and for
primary products, local content requirements for U.S. firms operating

in Mexico, migration policy, fishing rights, conflicts over oil and gas policy, etc. Mexican issues will become increasingly inter-related with domestic politics in the United States.

5) The countries and territories of the Caribbean region will continue to struggle, with little success probably, to achieve simul-taneously economic growth, improved equity, fuller employment, ex-panded political participation, and enhanced autonomy. The incom-patibility of all these goals in many Caribbean situations will be-come increasingly evident, posing serious issues for the region and for the United States.

6) Central America will continue to seethe until the long-estab-lished social order has been replaced by the institutionalization of a new power structure.

7) Throughout the region, and especially in the Caribbean coun-tries and in Argentina and Brazil, democratic institutions and prac-tices will continue to hold their appeal as the most promising basis for assuring stable, legitimate institutions, but the pressures of international and national economic exigencies will keep open the issue of democracy's viability in Latin America.

8) Latin America will continue to be a region free of a major all-out military conflict, but significant interstate conflicts and tensions, fueled by arms buildups, may erupt during the decade.

9) The crucial need to improve Latin America's agricultural productivity, especially of food, will become increasingly recog-nized throughout the Americas.

10) The issue of defining Puerto Rico's status, perennially ignored on the mainland, will force itself to national conscious-ness in the United States, in part because of Latin American pressure.

U.S. responses to Latin American and Caribbean trends

In general terms, the United States may respond to these regional dynamics in any of three ways: 1) by attempting to resist, i.e., to preserve as much of the hemispheric status quo as possible; 2) by working to restore a hemispheric "special relationship," i.e., to improve U.S.-Latin American relations at the expense of other interests and ties of the United States; or 3) to support a broad restructuring of international relations in ways conducive to the interests of the major Latin American countries but also of middle-tier developing countries in other regions.

An attempt to protect the status quo on the part of the United States would involve the imposition of protectionist tariffs, countervailing duties, quotas, and orderly marketing arrangements.

It would imply struggle over the repayment of debt, over remittances and repatriation of profits, over the rights and duties of multinationals, over immigration restrictions, over energy choices and proliferation; in short, over a broad agenda of international issues. Potential mutualities of interest between Latin America and the United States would go unrecognized and shared losses would be maximized. Latin Americans would increasingly link their grievances with other Third and Fourth World countries. The ambience for conducting U.S. foreign policy would deteriorate still more.

A second approach would be to try to revive a "special relationship" in the Western Hemisphere through a series of reinvigorated regional mechanisms: privileged U.S. access to Latin American commodities; assured opportunities for foreign investment; agreed purchases of Latin America's exported manufactures by the United States; preferential Latin American access to U.S. capital and technology; and orderly marketing arrangements to avert destructive trade competition. Many old Latin American hands are attracted by these concepts, even though most of them recognize that the lingo of "special relationship" is anathema for many Latin Americans who identify it with singling out the region for special rhetorical and/or interventionist attention, but for little else. These advocates of a regional policy that is more than rhetorical see the world as heading into a neo-mercantilist phase, and believe that the United States is blessed with a congenial set of partners for a set of geographically clustered economic-political groups. In this concept, the very economic dynamism and strength of the region converts itself into an asset in that it would help the United States construct a relatively powerful regional bloc.

The "special relationship" concept (apart from its lingo) should be criticized on two grounds, however. First, it is unlikely to appeal to the major Latin American nations, which have by now forged extensive and valuable international links that do not depend on the goodwill of the United States. Brazil, Mexico, Argentina, and other countries of the Americas are unlikely to give up the new sources of capital, technology, and other imports from the new markets they have developed throughout our world. Second, Latin American reluctance aside, the presumed advantages to the United States of such a regional accord are deceptive, for the process of regionalism and retaliation would leave the United States much worse off overall than it has been to date. The United States is far more involved in the world economy than it was in the 1930s or even in the 1950s and 1960s; we would lose the most from a retraction to the Western Hemisphere.

I strongly favor the third approach: to accommodate to Latin America's emergence and that of other middle-tier developing countries by working to restructure the international economic and political order so that their interests are recognized.* The

*In this section, I draw heavily on my previous work, jointly with Albert Fishlow, Latin America's Emergence: Toward a US Response. Headline Series #243, Foreign Policy Association (1979).

85

objective of U.S. policy toward Latin America and toward the developing countries more generally should be to help restructure international economic relations so that developing countries and already
industrialized ones can enjoy the benefits of generally expanding
international commerce.

How to achieve this aim in practice is not easily summarized
in a few words, of course. Suffice it to say that trade regimes and
agreements, monetary policies and institutional technology transfer
arrangements, codes of conduct for the role played by foreign direct
investment, immigration policies and agreements: all could be worked
out to the mutual advantage of the newly industrialized countries
and the established industrialized nations. (See Lowenthal and
Fishlow, Latin America's Emergence, pp. 52-70 for some details.)
Adjustments, sometimes painful for particular sectors, would be
necessary in the older industrialized countries like the United
States. Some concessions, perhaps costly in immediate terms, would
also be required from the newly industrialized countries. But
the long-term benefits for both could be very significant, in terms
of the direct consequences of expanding trade and investment and
also through cooperation on crucial issues such as energy, food,
and development.

Latin America, the United States, and the rest of the world

The central issues in U.S.-Latin American relations during the 1980s
will be conditioned by the direction this country takes at home.

If the United States reverses its decline, restores productivity, adapts to changing international comparative advantage, recog-
nizes the importance of immigrant labor for its economy, and more
generally accepts that it can lose hegemony without necessarily
sacrificing on other significant dimensions, then this country may
find Latin American nations and other key Third World countries
(China, India, Korea, Taiwan, Nigeria) are helpful allies.

The historic obstacle to the adoption by the United States of
policies favored by Latin American governments has always been
Big Business in the United States; the principal enemy of the
policy I am sketching out here might be organized labor. Traditionally, political alignments and their effects on U.S. foreign
policy toward Latin America and elsewhere may very well be challenged during the 1980s.

If, on the other hand, the United States enters a protectionist,
nationalist, assertive phase -- as may happen -- then Latin America
may pose tough and unpleasant challenges. One can imagine very
conflictful scenarios in the Western Hemisphere during the 1980s:
military intervention by the United States in Central America and
the Caribbean; intense clashes with Venezuela and Mexico over energy;
deepening conflicts with Brazil, Mexico, and other nations over

various economic issues; and increased links between Latin American
nations and other Third World countries, as well as other industrialized powers, at the expense of the United States.

Latin America has often had for the United States, like the
quality of the distorting mirror at the circus, a characteristic
of magnifying our society's traits out of all proportion, whether
noble or less so. The 1980s will present interesting questions
in that regard. Which of the national characteristics will be
stressed in the 1980s remains to be seen.

DISCUSSION

U.S. NATIONAL INTERESTS IN LATIN AMERICA

The two speakers, Abraham Lowenthal and Constantine Menges, did
share some common ground. Both agreed on the rapid, if uneven,
economic progress achieved in Latin America over the past 20 years,
and on the relatively high importance of hemispheric affairs compared with the claims of other regions. Both singled out Mexico
and the Caribbean for special attention.

They disagreed about the nature of the general challenges that
the United States confronts and the appropriate strategies of
response.

Both speakers regarded the economic problems of the Third
World as of pressing importance, requiring early and urgent attention, and involving major financial and political efforts on the
part of the rich countries as a whole. By implication both seemed
to suggest that since these global problems were unlikely to be
diminished in the next few years, the United States might directly
experience growing symptoms of Third World economic distress,
which would probably require very delicate bilateral negotiations
on specific issues. Illegal migration from the adjoining states
was discussed, and more generally it seemed that Latin America would
still be the region of the Third World where a faltering of the development process would most directly affect the United States.

The core of the discussion concerned major differences between
the two speakers on the scale and gravity of what might be termed
"the Marxist threat" in Latin America. Menges argued that vital
U.S. interests were at stake in the region, a standpoint that was
dramatized by his use of "best case" and "worst case" alternatives.
The "best case," which would be highly desirable from the standpoint
of U.S. national interests, would be the consolidation throughout
the Western Hemisphere of stable democracies capable of promoting

social justice. To this he contrasted a "worst case" outcome that would be extremely harmful to U.S. security interests, and that rested on what he described as a "domino theory." In his view, the Central American crisis is essentially the work of an extreme left terrorist conspiracy, sponsored by Cuba, which has succeeded in duping the West European Social Democrats, and perhaps the Mexican government, into believing that the process is one of popular national liberation to promote social justice and freedom. In the current phase of this conspiracy, the socially reforming government of El Salvador is, according to Menges, being subjected to political-military assault. Although the Carter administration is to be applauded for its backing of social reform in El Salvador, it has rashly tolerated a serious geopolitical threat to U.S. security because of its failure to give the Salvadoran security forces proper backing. Nicaragua may already, he thought, be on the verge of becoming a totalitarian Marxist police state. In consequence there is a substantial risk that El Salvador will follow Nicaragua, with Guatemala, and possibly Honduras, Costa Rica, and Panama, following the same road within a couple of years.

Already he would put the risk of a major extension of Communist insurgency into southern Mexico at around 20 percent. A "Communist-dominated" Central America would raise the risk of an upheaval in Mexico to, say, 70 percent, he added. Even though the Mexican left might well be crushed in these circumstances, the consequences for the United States would be extremely severe, with a possibility of floods of refugees crossing the Rio Grande, and of insecurity and disruption in Mexico spilling over into the domestic American arena. If this "worst case" scenario is as probable as Menges believed it to be, the major U.S. national interest in Latin America for the next few years would be, he deduced, to actively promote and strengthen democratic forces in the regions that are capable of turning back the left terrorist assault. To reinforce the strength of his conclusion, he argued that the resources required to mount an effective resistance would in any case be low. But it seems to follow from his analysis that even if the costs of resistance proved to be far higher than his present estimates, it would still be a vital U.S. national interest to reverse the tide in Central America.

Lowenthal described the above "worst case" scenario as a "parade of imaginary horribles." He attached lower probability than Menges to the sequence of events just outlined, and he considered that it would be against U.S. national interests to shape American policy in the region primarily with reference to such improbable hypotheticals, above all because this would distract attention from the far more pressing sources of difficulty for U.S. foreign policy in the region.

Lowenthal's paper emphasized international economic issues rather than political-military concerns; it stressed the significance of the major Latin American countries (Brazil, Mexico,

Venezuela, and Argentina) rather than Central America or Cuba; and it situated U.S. interests more in a North-South than an East-West context. Lowenthal laid more emphasis on responding to the distinctive national preoccupations of the major Latin American powers rather than necessarily requiring them to share U.S. pre-occupations and perceptions. Difficult tasks of persuasion and coordination lie ahead, if the international community as a whole is to respond constructively to such multifaceted and interrelated problems as Third World indebtedness, the security of supplies of essential commodities (notably food and energy), the preservation of open trading relationships, relatively free movement for capital and labor, and the promotion of the associated political values of pluralism, tolerance, and openness. American sensitivity to Latin American susceptibilities is all the more important since it would probably be necessary to ask for greater responsiveness on the part of Latin neighbors to the susceptibilities of U.S. public opinion, which is becoming concerned by the perceived effects of increasingly competitive industrial imports from the Third World and the apparent employment threat posed by weakly controlled immigration.

Concerning "containment," Lowenthal indicated more confidence in the Mexican government's ability to tame and co-opt revolutionary movements in Central America. The best way, he argued, to reinforce the Mexican capacity to manage the situation would be to cooperate with them in easing the social and economic problems that most concern the Mexican administration and that threaten to damage the climate for U.S.-Mexican collaboration. It would be quite counter-productive to try to press the Mexican administration to fall into line behind American worries about the security situation.

One member of the audience asked Lowenthal how serious the situation would have to become in Central America before the gravity of the threat to U.S. national interests became inescapable. Lowenthal's answer followed by extension from his analysis of the markets that even Marxist regimes will need if they are to resolve any of their acute internal problems. For this reason the "Cuban security threat" does not rank very high in Lowenthal's list of America's regional priorities. If the United States makes a major issue of Cuban advisers or the Cuban military threat, then it creates a major foreign policy problem for itself.

Menges disagreed, itemizing the number of countries (especially in Africa) in which there has been substantial Cuban military intervention. Cuban influence in Latin America promotes civil strife, and therefore contributes as much to the undermining of human rights as the actions of right-wing governments. The highest priority that should shape American foreign policy is the promotion of political freedom, which might be attained through gradualism in the case of right-wing regimes. Once freedom is lost to the totalitarian left, on the other hand, it is extremely difficult to restore. With regard to socioeconomic deterioration, that can be, and has been, reversed. Therefore, although not dissenting

about the socioeconomic problems of Latin America, and not advo-
cating improper or military forms of intervention to combat Cuban
influence, Menges persisted with his view that America's highest
priority in the region should be to oppose Cuban and left terrorist
expansionism, which he presented as the contemporary equivalent
of 1930s' fascism. It is necessary to proceed simultaneously on
several related fronts to defeat the left. Politically it is
important to offer a democratic, and not just repressive, alternative to Communist success, and on the economic front prudent
assistance is required to help threatened economies adapt to the
global economic crisis.

It is notable that Menges's way of framing the issues implies
a high degree of American domestic unity in the pursuit of foreign
policy goals and would also require considerable assertiveness
abroad. These conditions were met in the early 1960s, but there
is considerable uncertainty about whether either the internal or
the international context will permit them to be re-created in the
1980s. Even if these obstacles can be overcome, it is not clear
whether Central America will provide the most favorable setting
for a reassertion of American liberal leadership.

With these themes as the focus of debate, other issues of potential significance received scant attention. The exclusive
focus on military issues of either an "ex-imperial" or "Cold War"
variety overshadowed consideration of other types of military
conflict (e.g., over border disputes, access to national resources,
or denying sanctuary to political adversaries). In particular
there is the question of Mexican oil, access to which could easily
become a vital strategic necessity for the United States if Middle
East supplies are cut off. When Mexicans read of the Iran-Iraq
War, the Rapid Deployment Force, or the incumbent governor of
Texas, they naturally ask themselves how militarily secure their
own natural resources may be. If "worst case" scenarios are to be
the basis for judgments of national interest, energy-related crises
would seem worthy of comparison with the "domino theory." Such
security worries of America's neighbor may be more "unreal" than
the concerns expressed by Menges, but they are no less fervently
held, and may therefore affect American interests to an extent
that is not currently foreseen.

Laurence Whitehead

AFRICA

U.S. NATIONAL INTERESTS IN AFRICA

William J. Foltz

"National interest" is a notoriously slippery concept, and ringing
declarations that a particular policy ought to be followed because
it is clearly "in the national interest" rightly induce skeptical
frowns from sophisticated audiences. National interest is particularly slippery when applied to an area of the world in which the
United States does not have a long-standing and tested policy tradition or a broad basis of public understanding. Such, unfortunately, is the case with Africa, an area toward which the United
States for most of its history has had no policy, and when it
began to notice Africa seriously came up with two, baptized "glo-
balist" and "regionalist." Nor does the American public provide
much guidance. On any national opinion poll about one-quarter of
the respondents will have no opinion on any African issue while an
additional tenth will reveal confusion on a scale to match that of
former Vice President Agnew, who once made an impassioned speech
at a meeting of the National Security Council based on the premise
that the whites of South Africa had unilaterally declared independence from Britain in 1965.

    Absent such a clear policy tradition and broad understanding,
one might best seek American national interests in a more general
understanding of the United States' evolving domestic situation
and role in the world. (As I shall argue, such a global starting
point does not excuse the analyst or policymaker from looking at
regional specifics when considering how best to advance those
interests.) Implicit in this approach is the assumption that American interests anywhere change as American society changes, as the
nation's international role changes, and as the interests and actions
of others change.

    To begin with the obvious, the United States is a profoundly
capitalist country that by and large has prospered under the international order it helped construct out of the wreckage of World
War II. Its conservatism in international affairs stems less from
any ideological conviction or inner spirit of the American people
than from its pragmatic interest in conserving a world order under

which it has done well. With few exceptions, radical departures in international arrangements are viewed more as potential risks than opportunities. Among the exceptions has been American support for dismantling formal Western political empires in the Third World, a change whose risks have been rendered acceptable by its consonance with traditional American political values and the expectation that the new nations could be drawn into a pattern of relationships advantageous to American economic and political interests. Constructing and maintaining such relationships without benefit of formal political control has preoccupied a generation of statesmen. In a sometimes turbulent international environment including serious challenges from the Soviet Union, it is no wonder that policy discussions of Third World issues have been dominated by the code word "stability." For many Americans stability has appeared as the summum bonum of international relationships and the ideal goal of domestic policies in countries with which the United States does business.

In an area like Africa, which remains peripheral to the main focus of U.S. international involvements and responsibilities, and which is not perceived (rightly or wrongly) by most thoughtful Americans as an area offering great opportunities, "stability" of core relationships and areas would not seem an unreasonable goal for American policy. Unfortunately, "stability" is hardly the first word that comes to mind when one thinks about Africa in the 1980s. In addition to the by now familiar patterns of coups and regime reversals, several longer-term trends will materially alter the African environment in which the United States, like other nations, will have to pursue its interests.

Trends in the '80s

The first of these trends is the spread of armaments on the African continent and the increased ability of some African states to put these arms to effective use. Since 1963, real spending on arms by African states has doubled every five years, and there is no indication that the rate of acquisition is falling off, now that the Soviet Union has replaced France and the United States as principal arms peddler to the continent. More important than the rate of acquisition of material, or even the amount of money diverted from civilian to military uses, is the fact that a few African countries have now passed the threshold at which they are capable of effective military offensives against foreign targets. For the first time, some African armies are capable of overthrowing a government that is not their own. The 1977 Somali invasion of the Ogaden, repulsed only by the introduction of Cuban troops, and the successful Tanzanian invasion of Uganda in 1979 have demonstrated a new capability to project force, as has the intervention of Libyan armored forces a thousand kilometers from their own border in the capital of Chad. Although each of these invasions depended on extra-African provisions of arms, they were acts of independent state power by

African regimes pursuing what they considered to be their own national interests. Nigeria and Zimbabwe are other sub-Saharan states that possess the capability to project effective military force beyond their borders, something that previously had been the privilege of white-ruled states and of extra-African intervention forces. The increased effectiveness of some African armies will further restrict the scope for old-fashioned gunboat (or paratroop) diplomacy by foreign powers. There will be an increasing number of areas in Africa in which outsiders must consider the possibility of taking significant losses if they try to shoot their way in.

The growth of military power reflects a broader pattern of increased differentiation among African states, pointing both to the emergence of a few subregional powers and the collapse of others into abject poverty. In the past, while great differences have existed among African states, the more favored ones have not possessed the absolute level of economic, military, or diplomatic resources necessary to intervene effectively by themselves, either to help or to harm, in other African states. When they have done so, they have acted in concert with extra-African powers. More recently, Nigeria, Libya, and Tanzania have been the most venturesome in asserting strong leadership roles, and their rivalries have erupted in only slightly veiled form at recent Organization of African Unity meetings. Zimbabwe, Kenya, Algeria, and a post-Houphouet Ivory Coast are other potential contenders for local leadership roles.

The other side of the coin consists of those areas of Africa that are becoming regional, if not international, basket cases. Chad and Uganda qualify already, and it would not be hard to find others to add to the sorry list. They are distinguished neither by ideology nor by colonial history, nor even by natural endowments. What is distinctive about these cases, Chad most clearly, is that they have become the setting for the acting out of rivalries between neighboring African powers. Such rivalries are likely increasingly to become the principal stuff of intra-African politics and to dominate the more trivial cleavages, such as those between francophones and anglophones and those based on rhetorical adherence to ideological formulations. This would represent a substantial transformation of intra-African politics away from issues based on extra-continental influence and heritage toward those based on regional power realities.

The dominant power in the southern African region will continue to be the Republic of South Africa. If states to the north have increased their military capabilities, so has the government of P.W. Botha, and no combination of forces from black Africa is going to make a military dent on the Republic for the foreseeable future. That is not the principal issue, however. More important to the future of South Africa is the continued rise in the absolute level of power of its black population, at least to the point at which South African blacks are able to withhold widespread acquiescence

to any social and political order from whose construction popular
black leaders are excluded. This is likely to remain a negative
power, a power to refuse, and will for considerable time fall short
of the relative power necessary to control. But it will be enough
at a minimum to keep the South African political cauldron simmering
domestically and sending off the occasional blasts of steam required
to fuel international concern. This seems likely to be true almost
irrespective of which of the presently discussed range of policies
the South African government seeks to implement. The economic role
of blacks is now too central and too complex to permit a return to
the successful repression of the 1960s without inflicting serious
damage to the South African economy and its military preparedness.
Nor do any reforms yet adumbrated possess either the qualitative
or quantitative dimensions necessary to buy black acquiescence.
One consequence of this dilemma is likely to be considerable upheaval in white South African politics, including the possibility
that the South African military will abandon its present position
as the power behind the throne to move out front and overtly take
the reins of power. Were they to do so they would presumably dis-
cover what other African military politicians have discovered,
i.e., that their options and resources are no better than those of
the civilians they have ousted.

Perhaps paradoxically, struggle for influence and leadership
among black African states will likely assure that South Africa
remains high on the international agenda. It is the one surefire
rallying point for Pan-African diplomatic cooperation. While as in
the past much of this Pan-African effort will be talk, and the most
virulent talk will come from those states safely distant from the
immediate arena of conflict, it will also include more tangible
support for exile groups. Even the talk has its effect on black
opinion and actions within South Africa. Although a Namibia settlement would provide some immediate relief for Western nations desir-
ous to avoid implementing painful measures against South Africa,
nations and corporations seeking to continue doing business both
north and south of the Limpopo will face problems if they do not
observe basic rules of discretion in dealing with Pretoria.

Domestic American political interests

What, then, are the implications of such unstable developments for
specific national interests of the United States? The first such
interest to look at is the most fundamental: our own domestic political tranquility. Perhaps fortunately, Africa as a whole is not a
source of impassioned division within the American body politic and
is unlikely to become one. That is not to say that sharp cleavages
of opinion do not arise over African policy, merely that those
cleavages usually derive from more general ideological positions
and not from specific interests in African events for their own
sakes. For most Americans and American politicians, Africa as a
whole does not enjoy enough salience to generate disruptive political

passions unless it becomes attached to issues that do exercise people: stopping Cubans or CIA dirty tricks, for example. Several lobbies for African interests do exist, and many of them -- the African-American Institute, TransAfrica, and the Washington Office on Africa, for example -- are doing commendable educational jobs. Within the black community interest in Africa and things African continues to increase. Nevertheless, Africa as a whole is highly unlikely to enjoy the single-minded, effective support of a lobby such as those active on behalf of Israel and Greece, for the simple reason that Africa provides a multiplicity of clients with often competitive or conflicting interests and needs. The same is not true, however, with regard to South Africa. There the fundamental racial issue arouses too many echoes of America's own deep dilemma for passions to remain dormant. There, also, the issues, seen from far enough away, take on the simplicity of black and white. If one does not know precisely what one is for, it is easy to tell what one is against. On South African issues black leadership opinion carries weight within the American black community as a whole and increasingly, through the Congressional Black Caucus, in the House of Representatives as well. No administration can cavalierly ignore that opinion without paying some price in other areas of immediate domestic concern.

This structure of domestic political interests suggests two principles for prudent management of American policy. First, with regard to Africa as a whole, beware the temptation to act out ideological proclivities with little regard to the facts of an African situation. (The Carter administration erred on both sides of this principle, with some of its spokesmen blithely denying the clearly anti-Soviet aspect of much of its southern African policy and others seizing every opportunity to turn local African conflict into an East-West showdown.) Second, recognize that in South Africa as perhaps nowhere else in the world the issue of human rights has a direct domestic connection. Policies begun in defiance of this are likely to be paralyzed before they can be carried through, or to entail heavy costs for America's own domestic political order.

Domestic American economic interests

In overall quantitative terms, Africa plays but a small role in America's domestic economic interests; nevertheless, Africa supplies a few commodities that are essential to the American economy. For most of the postwar period, total trade with sub-Saharan Africa has represented about 4 percent of total U.S. foreign commerce, with South Africa accounting for one-quarter of the amount. These percentage figures have been remarkably stable in the aggregate and seem unlikely to change dramatically during the 1980s. Total U.S. direct investment in the region amounts to about $3.8 billion, of which South Africa accounts for slightly over half, a proportion that has been growing slowly over the last few years, due principally to stagnation of American investment in tropical Africa. American corporations have lagged behind those of other OECD countries in prospecting African markets and developing investment opportunities, and few major company plans view Africa as one of their growth areas. Since the U.S. trade balance with Africa, as with the rest of the world, remains in deficit, there ought clearly to be an interest in encouraging more aggressive corporate attention to African economic opportunities, as well as in assisting African countries to develop the human and material infrastructure that will create such opportunities.

More prominent in terms of immediate American interests is Africa's role as a supplier of oil and gas and of a few key minerals. As is well known, Nigeria is the United States' second-largest supplier of oil imports. In the first half of 1980, the three principal African exporters (Nigeria, Libya, and Algeria) together supplied 27 percent of American oil imports as against 22 percent from Saudi Arabia and the United Arab Emirates. Both Algeria and Nigeria are potentially major suppliers of LNG to U.S. markets. Southern Africa, from Zaire's Shaba Province south, is a major repository of minerals essential to modern industry. Of these, chromium (from South Africa and Zimbabwe), cobalt (from Zaire and Zambia), manganese (South Africa and Gabon), and platinum group metals (South Africa) are of enough industrial importance that the United States cannot lightly undertake policies that would put their provision at risk for extended periods of time.

The phrase "resource war" is much in the air these days, and many have urged that the United States take extreme steps to assure itself control over crucial minerals and energy sources. Most of this talk is either hysterical or self-serving and proposes nostrums more costly than the ills they seek to prevent. Prudent policy based on America's national interest (as opposed, for example, to the interest of a particular corporation) must begin with the goal of maximizing long-term access at market rates to the minerals the United States and its allies need. Access must of course be distinguished from ownership, which is not a matter of national interest, at least not the U.S. national interest. Long-term access requires that the United States enjoy at least tolerable relations with whatever groups control the states in which the minerals are located. With regard to South Africa, one can reasonably disagree over what the most prudent time horizon is for access planning, and therefore over what is likely to be the skin color of those groups in control of the state, but the latter point is hardly at issue in the other African countries involved. Even with regard to South Africa, it would seem imprudent in the extreme to base any long-term planning on policies that systematically alienate the principal black groups. Access further requires that political and physical conditions on the ground will not be so disrupted that production and evacuation is made impossible. Again, to plan prudently, one might consider it strongly in America's own interest to facilitate overall economic development and political tranquility throughout the extended southern African area. If that is too

much to ask, at least one should design policies so as not to make
things worse over the long run.

Two other points are made by those worried about a "resource
war." The first is that any spread of Marxist-Leninist ideology
would threaten the West's access. To this, one can only oppose the
historical record that so far, no African state of any ideological
(or dermatological) pigmentation has refused to sell any Western
country any available commodity when offered market prices. African states that consider themselves Marxist or Socialist are among
the most aggressive bidders for Western involvement in their economies and certainly for Western markets for their products. The
second point is more worrisome: What about African states directly
under Soviet control? Will they not join in a resource boycott to
bring the West to its knees? Part of an answer must be that in
those countries where the Soviets are presumed to have some influence, nothing of the sort has yet happened. But beyond that, no
one would deny that the United States has an interest in preventing
major African countries from being "controlled" by the U.S.S.R.
The question is how do you do it. Much of the rest of this paper
will address that question.

Security interests

For the great powers Africa has traditionally held little intrinsic
strategic interest. In strategic terms, it has historically been
an obstacle -- or a way station -- on the way to somewhere important, a launching pad for attacks elsewhere, a source of military
resources (particularly cannon fodder), and occasionally a convenient place for major powers to act out rivalries without coming to
blows in areas closer to home where the cost would be higher. The
sea routes around Africa have historically held more strategic
interest than the continent itself.

Current great-power security concerns in Africa are running
true to historic form; the continent is viewed as a convenient
launching pad for forays into the Middle East and as a base for
protecting important sea lanes. Africa's, or more precisely the
Horn of Africa's, attraction as a launching pad for Middle Eastern
expeditions derives from the simple fact that it is not in the
Middle East. Facilities in the Middle East, it is feared, would
further destabilize that region, or involve us with local clients
who might use us for purposes of which we would disapprove. The
same problems can arise with military facilities on the Horn, of
course. Their implantation in Africa instead of the Middle East
makes sense only if the political costs are less and if prudent
action is taken to keep these costs low.

The direct introduction of American military forces may provoke
reactions that end up worsening the United States' overall strategic position. The greatest such risk is facilitating the Soviets'

acquisition of something they have never had, major strategic bases on the African continent. It is striking that even the most radical states have resisted giving the Soviets such facilities. Where the Soviets have enjoyed lower-level privileges, such as operating occasional ocean surveillance flights and naval-bunkering facilities, the African states involved have themselves been under a security threat from Western-associated forces -- Guinee in the late 1960s and early '70s, Angola and Ethiopia today.

The United States does not benefit when African regional rivalries are exacerbated and polarized in terms of great-power alliances and military backing. Such a situation provides the greatest possible opportunity for the Soviets to acquire military assets that would be immediately significant in the East-West balance.

Since, in the Horn of Africa, the United States has already committed itself to establishing military "facilities" at Mombasa (Kenya) and Berbera (Somalia), it should staff and operate them with the greatest restraint and discretion. It should also make a major effort to limit Somali military adventures in the Ogaden. Neither of these will be simple. In southern Africa, American or other Western forces' use of South Africa's Simonstown naval base would almost certainly provide the Soviets with the arguments they need to establish major bases in Mozambique and Angola. In geostrategic terms, such mutual escalation would constitute a net loss for the West.

Great-power security issues cannot always be neatly divorced from local African security issues. It is only prudent, however, that the United States not try to impose a great-power dimension on disputes that are essentially local in origin and can be settled in terms of local realities. The two attacks on Zaire's Shaba Province by the former Katangese Gendarmes are cases in point. They are most accurately explained, as they were ultimately resolved, in terms of the complex relations between two unstable African states, Angola and Zaire. Similarly, one sure way of entrenching the Soviet military position in Angola, and of contributing to the instability of neighbors like Zaire and Zambia, would be for the United States to begin providing military aid for Jonas Savimbi's UNITA. Our interest is in reducing the Cuban and Soviet presence in Angola and in helping all Angolans create a stable and productive economy, not in creating a dramatic stage on which, as one U.S. senator hyperbolically wrote recently, "Each day Savimbi's forces strike further blows against the pernicious Soviet doctrine that the world is somehow 'destined' to go the Soviet way."

Real African security problems are difficult indeed, and it is decidedly to our advantage that they be solved as close to the ground as possible and in terms of local realities. Unlike the Soviet Union, we profit from what most Africans want: a decrease in foreign military involvement and an increase in local stability and economic activity. If we are to compete with the Soviets in Africa, our advantage is to keep the competition political and economic, not military -- the only dimension on which the Soviets can match, or perhaps overmatch, us. Africa provides an abundance of opportunities for political and economic initiatives, which are likely to provide a much greater contribution to "stability" and continued "access" than will any direct military involvements. Effective action is impossible without some identification with major African political and economic interests. Where we have acted boldly and patiently to midwife change -- as in Zimbabwe and, one hopes, ultimately in Namibia -- we have succeeded in blocking Soviet influence and producing changes clearly to our long-run advantage.

Political interests in Africa

The overall task of American diplomacy in Africa is to create an environment on the continent in which our long-term economic interests can flourish, and outside the continent to achieve some measure of African support for our other enterprises. At a minimum, we should strive to avoid creating unnecessarily hostile relations, which will give us a group of hostile nations nipping at our heels as we try to attend to serious international business. The Carter administration deserves generally high marks in this respect, though the previous administration had already begun, notably through William Scranton's patient diplomacy, to repair some of the ravages of Moynihanism at the United Nations. However satisfying to the ego of those who make the speeches, the United States serves no national interest by putting itself "in opposition" to the Third World. There are many precedents for expecting that most African states will be among the most understanding and helpful members of the ill-matched agglomerate called the Third World. If a U.S. administration feels domestic pressure to lash out in diplomatic rebuke of Africa, the United Nations may be the worst forum for doing so -- if only because of General Assembly voting rules.

The many differences among African states must be recognized in American diplomacy. "Africa" is not a single international actor, nor does it follow a single line of interest, nor indeed is there a single "true" African policy on most international issues. Nevertheless, the United States has a clear interest in dealing with all of Africa and occasionally with Africa as a whole. In particular it must avoid trying to enforce a split in Africa between "moderates" and "radicals," between "our guys" and "their guys." Such a split falsifies reality on the ground and acts against American interests in two ways. First, the United States can do better. Splitting Africa means consigning some states into a tighter Soviet embrace than we -- or the African states involved -- would prefer, and at the same time denying ourselves diplomatic and possibly economic access. It is a mistake that the Soviets do not make. Second, if we are serious about backing our friends and creating and confounding African enemies, we are going to be very busy and are going to be committing substantial resources, in

some cases to highly erratic regimes that will have little incentive to put their own houses in order. African cultures are filled
with devious mechanisms through which clients trade surface defer-
ence for actual control over their patrons. More realistically,
a policy of dividing Africa would proceed by fits and starts, and
we would in fact end up abandoning some of "our guys" when they
got into serious trouble at home or abroad. The United States
would thus end up with no policy at all, but would have acquired
a few dedicated enemies in the process. Splitting Africa is the
counsel of those without the patience to think through and act
in a complicated world. One may accept that it is the stuff of
which campaign speeches are made. It is not the stuff of which
serious policy can be constructed.

Dealing with Africa as a whole means that we work with the
unfolding pattern of multiple cleavages in intra-African politics
and avoid hardening them into a single ideological divide. It
means recognizing that we may want to provide military assistance
to a variety of African states having legitimate security concerns;
that economic aid can properly be used to open diplomatic as well
as commercial doors, and that refusing it to a Mozambique, for
example, serves no policy purpose at all. Perhaps the most obvious step to take is recognition of Angola, to give that government
-- which has greatly helped Western initiatives in dealing with
Namibia -- greater freedom of maneuver in dealing with its principal outside supporters and in working toward the internal reconciliation that alone can stabilize this troubled country and open
up its extensive resources to international commerce.

Finally, what are our political interests in the Republic of
South Africa? We are engaged by our past actions in that most
troublesome country, but we lack great leverage on any party. By
the nature of our engagement and our domestic political pressures,
we also lack great freedom of maneuver. It is easy to say what we
do want: peaceful, steady progress toward equal political and
social rights for all South Africans. It seems much too late in
South Africa's history for that to occur. There may, however,
be many tactical and procedural advantages to continuing to press
constantly for such progress and to be seen doing so. It is certainly in the national interest, and in their own long-run interests, for American corporations to participate in such pressure,
at a minimum by applying seriously the augmented Sullivan principles in their own operations. It is in the nature of business
corporations, however, that without pressure and support from
American national leadership, they will follow a short-term calculus and let their efforts flag, particularly since they are not
likely to be rewarded by warm words of praise from South African
blacks or by an extended period of social calm.

Since it lacks the ability to produce the outcomes it desires
in South Africa, U.S. policy might best concentrate on what outcomes it wants to avoid. I suggest three. Obviously, we want

103

to avoid South Africa's being controlled by a power hostile to us.
The Soviet Union has been interested in South Africa since at least
1922; it is perhaps the only part of the continent that they consistently take seriously and to whose principal nationalist movement
they have given unflagging support. Second, we want to avoid
creating another diplomatic Israel, a beleaguered outpost for whose
security we have become responsible. Strong identification with
the white minority and abandoning the cause of black nationalism to
the Soviets could well produce just such a result. Finally, we want
to avoid widespread physical destruction of South Africa and the
southern African region. We have, thus, in common with most South
Africans an interest in limiting the violence through which change
takes place. We have an interest in not making this a place where
East and West act out their hostilities militarily, and furthermore
in keeping as much of the struggle as possible internal to South
Africa. At a minimum, this will require continued U.S. engagement
and rapport with all South African forces, groups, and shades of
opinion. Further afield, it will require a high level of concerned
Western diplomacy and cooperation with South Africa's black neighbors. At home, it will require political restraint to avoid making
that complex land a setting for an American moral drama.

In some ways Africa presents a somber setting for the pursuit
of American national interest. It is not, I think, a continent
where there are vast opportunities for gain that will redound dramatically to the benefit either of the American standard of living or
to the reelection campaigns of American politicians. It does,
however, provide numerous opportunities to make mistakes, the most
obvious of which stem from attempting to impose an external ideological mold on African realities and from attempting to seek short-
run, flashy advantage. In the long run, with which national
interest must be primarily concerned, the picture is much less
somber. And the African long run is more important to us than
threats from any present danger on that continent. The United
States needs little out of Africa, economically or politically,
that Africans are not, for their own purposes, willing to provide,
if only they are offered fair exchange. For the moment, what is
required from Washington is a difficult combination of involvement,
understanding, support, and restraint, in our own national interest
and in that of most Africans.

THE RELATIONSHIP BETWEEN U.S. NATIONAL INTERESTS
AND VARIOUS COUNTRIES AND/OR AREAS IN AFRICA

James O.C. Jonah

U.S. interest and Africa

In the year of revolutions in Europe -- 1848 -- Lord Palmerston,
the eminent foreign minister of England, came under severe criticism from two main quarters: the conservatives pictured him as an
agent of the revolutionary forces in Europe while the radicals ac-
cused him of not doing enough to enhance the cause of revolution.
Furthermore, the alliances he fashioned with various states in
Europe were seen as too opportunistic. Faced with this contradictory criticism, Lord Palmerston, on March 1, 1848, rose in the House
of Commons to defend his foreign policy initiatives. In doing so,
he uttered memorable words that represent for many the quintes-
sence of realpolitik. He observed:

> ...therefore I say that it is a narrow policy to suppose
> that this country or that is to be marked out as the eter-
> nal ally or the perpetual enemy of England. We have no
> eternal allies and we have no perpetual enemies. Our inter-
> ests are eternal and perpetual and those interests it is
> our duty to follow.

In the circumstances of the shifting alliances between states,
whether in the context of the so-called balance-of-power philosophy
or in more modern times, it is a simple matter to agree with Lord
Palmerston that nations indeed have no eternal allies or perpetual
enemies. Less certain is Palmerston's second assertion that a
nation's interests are eternal and perpetual. Is this really the
case? If so, how do we discern it or how do we best determine what
are a nation's real interests? It is a common practice for foreign
policy analysts to assume, as did Palmerston, that a state's national
interests are clearly discernible and immutable. It is this common
assumption that often presents great difficulties in foreign policy
analyses.

In order to be able to determine precisely what U.S. national
interests are with respect to Africa, one needs a careful analysis

of by whom and in what circumstances such national interests are being defined. We are aware that enunciation of U.S. national interests in specific circumstances can vary from one administration to another. Political parties often present differing perceptions of what national interests should be. Even within a political party there may well be differing attitudes toward a definition of U.S. national interests and most significantly, the political persuasion of the president of the United States as well as his secretary of state and national security adviser may influence the determination of national interests. Consequently, it has not been a promising exercise to state precisely what are the national interests of the United States. What one can reasonably do is to present one's own perception of what ought to be the national interests of the United States. Such a perception is necessarily based on one's knowledge and understanding of the history, hopes, and aspirations of the American people and the rich legacy of previous political leadership. There remains the great risk, however, that one's perception may vary greatly from the reality.

A broad guideline to assist us in formulating U.S. national interest was offered by Lord Palmerston's statement mentioned above. He had begun the statement by observing that the England of his time was to be the champion of justice and right and that she ought to give the weight of her moral sanction and support wherever she thought that justice was and wherever she thought that wrong had been done. The combination of national interests and moral principles made a deep impression on the British people at that time. It is not farfetched to say that in the African context, a widespread perception of U.S. national interests is of a state whose fundamental interests, based on its own colonial history, ought to be to defend the weak against the strong and to give succor and refuge to those who suffer deprivation and neglect.

Promotion of human rights

But here again we face some real problems. It is no secret that there is a wide divergence of views among the American political leadership as to whether the vigorous promotion of human rights is a major national interest of the United States. Some argue that the ideal of the Declaration of Independence and the civil liberties enshrined in the U.S. Constitution make it incumbent on the United States to defend and promote human rights everywhere. Others fervently believe that the advocacy and promotion of human rights abroad could work against U.S. national interests. Proponents of this point of view are too ready to pinpoint specific instances when vigorous advocacy of human rights has resulted in the toppling of a government friendly to the United States and the assumption of power by forces hostile to U.S. interests. But even those who may agree that the promotion of human rights is a valid national interest of the United States may argue against its rigid application in specific situations. They may disagree with the linkage of

human rights observance with agreement on trade policies or the
pursuit of negotiations to limit strategic weapons. In a sense,
some advocates of human rights may not agree that it is useful or
proper for the United States to apply reward and punishment in
relation to the observance and nonobservance of human rights.

From the African perspective, there is some confusion as to
whether the United States indeed believes in the promotion of
human rights. On the one hand, they observe that strong actions
are taken in certain areas in reaction to violations of basic
human rights, yet in those situations that are of highest importance
to Africans, Africans do not perceive the United States as taking
a leading role. Consequently, the credibility of the United States
suffers. For example, many Africans noted the extensive American
efforts to organize a boycott against the Moscow Olympic games
because of the Soviet involvement in Afghanistan when, only four
years earlier, the United States joined others in criticizing the
Africans when they sought to organize a boycott against the Montreal
Olympic games on account of apartheid in South Africa.

Those Africans who believe it is in the national interest of
the United States to defend and promote human rights everywhere
find it difficult to understand U.S. foreign policy vis-a-vis
apartheid in South Africa. In terms of official pronouncements,
the United States has opposed the policy of apartheid, yet has not
joined in the African call for mandatory economic sanctions to help
put an end to the policy. What many Africans fear is that a higher
priority is given to the economic and strategic interests of the
United States than to the elimination of apartheid. Explanations
to the effect that economic sanctions will do more harm to the
nonwhite populations have not been found convincing to most Africans.

Strategic interests of the United States in Africa

What indeed are the strategic interests of the United States in
Africa? Obviously, there can be no simple answer to this question.
In certain areas of the continent some African countries may well
see a U.S. military presence as a bulwark against hostile forces
and foreign intervention. In such circumstances, they may want to
provide military facilities for U.S. military forces in exchange
for arms transfers or military guarantees.

The grave risk for the United States in such instances is
that what in one area of Africa might be perceived as enlightened
national interest can be harshly judged by other African countries
as a form of neocolonialism and reckless involvement of Africa in
great-power struggles or confrontations. By and large, most African
countries would wish to keep military competition and rivalry
between the great powers out of the continent. The provision of
military bases or its modern variant -- military facilities -- is

still not looked upon with favor by the majority of African countries. Even though there are circumstances when a particular
African country may call for foreign military assistance in time
of national peril, the general unpopularity of outside military
involvement should not be minimized.

To what extent is it prudent for the United States to disregard
African sensibilities against great-power military involvement in
Africa? It is easy enough for some to argue that Africans are naive
to believe that the continent could be isolated from the strategic
contest between the great powers and that it is of vital importance
for the United States to look after its own national strategic
interests. For example, does the gravity of the situation in the
Persian Gulf region or what has been called the "Arc of Crises"
warrant the U.S. military involvement in the Horn of Africa? The
answer will require a careful analysis of the cost of such involvement. Much would depend on the scale of U.S. military involvement.
Nevertheless, the repercussions could be incalculable. It would
appear more appropriate and perhaps in the better interest of the
United States if efforts were redoubled to reduce, if not eliminate,
all foreign military presence in Africa, particularly that of the
greatest powers.

One may legitimately ask why the majority of African states
appear to have tolerated the presence of Cuban military forces in
Angola and the Cuban and Soviet military presence in Ethiopia.
Here again, there is no uniform African perspective. Africans,
after all, are not unique in the great human drama. There are
Africans who have been vocal in taking stands for or against such
military presence and involvement. By and large, however, the
majority African attitude toward the Cuban military presence in
Angola can be explained in the context of the situation in southern
Africa, particularly the continuing civil strife in Angola and
Namibia. It is fair to say that Africans saw the introduction of
Cuban military forces in Angola as a deterrent to South Africa's
military activity against Angola and its continuing presence in
Namibia. Western assertions that the Cuban forces are surrogates
for Soviet "imperialism" have not been convincing to many African
observers. The tolerance for Soviet military advisers in Ethiopia
may well be compared to the tolerance shown by many Africans to the
presence of French military forces in some francophone African
countries.

Economic interests

Many Africans find it hard to grasp fully the economic or strategic
interests of the United States in South Africa when compared to the
opportunities available in the rest of Africa. Perhaps U.S. foreign
policy analysts have not yet fully elaborated on those specific
interests that warrant continuing U.S. economic involvement in South
Africa. What are the controlling factors? Are U.S. or Western

investments the major factor, or is South Africa's significant leverage in the crucial gold bullion market the real key? Whatever it is, Africans believe U.S. interests would be better served by reducing the present U.S. economic involvement in South Africa. African states believe, moreover, that the national interest of the United States should lead to U.S. assistance in their development efforts.

Most important developments in the 1980s

Africans are unanimous in hoping that the United States will continue to lend its strong support to the drive to end all vestiges of colonialism in Africa. In this connection, it is hoped that South Africa will be encouraged to proceed expeditiously in the implementation of the U.N. plan for Namibia. Indeed, it will be a fatal mistake to allow developments to move away from the basic principle of free and fair elections in Namibia as the basis of its independence. That Namibia will be independent in the '80s is no longer in doubt. The question is whether independence will be achieved peacefully, as envisaged in the U.N. plan, or by revolutionary methods. Africans believe that it should be in the vital national interest of the United States to ensure that South Africa cooperates closely with the United Nations in the achievement of Namibian independence.

Peaceful change versus revolutionary change

Peaceful change versus revolutionary change will be in the balance in the 1980s. What the United States does or does not do in Namibia or in South Africa could tip the scale in one direction or the other. Africans expect the United States to stand on the side of constructive, peaceful change. This will require wisdom, statesmanship, and understanding. It is of the greatest importance that U.S. policymakers strive always to take the long-range view. There are times when it will be tempting in the short run to support local insurgents against a government not sympathetic to U.S. policy. It will be equally risky to give aid and comfort to a repressive and nondemocratic government that provides short-range stability in terms of U.S. policy considerations. In this context, Africans have clearly indicated that they wish to see increased U.S. support for the government of Angola and the denial of any support to those forces presently challenging the authority of the central government. Africa will not look with favor on any policy that deviates from this common expectation. At the same time, the United States ought to make clear that it stands ready to assist those countries that have opted for democratic government. Nigeria and Uganda, in their return to civilian rule, have set an example for many African countries. This is why there is urgent need for the United States to re-evaluate its economic assistance priorities in Africa. More support should be offered to those forces struggling to establish democratic politics and a more open society. Educational institutions and basic agriculture should be of the highest priority in the economic assistance of the United States.

The 1980s will undoubtedly witness significant changes in South Africa itself. This will be a major test for U.S. national interests. No one should minimize the determination that will be shown by the present leadership of South Africa to defend, perhaps at all costs, the present institutions of that country. But it is clear to many Africans that in an era of decolonization and of growing aspirations, the policy of apartheid can no longer be endured. It must therefore be expected that the black populations of South Africa will show increasing resistance to the present policy during the 1980s. How can the United States meet such a challenge? It will be necessary to urge the present government of South Africa to adopt measures that will facilitate peaceful change with a view to a greater democratization of South African society. Failure to do this will, in the long run, only jeopardize the vital interests of the 4.3 million white South Africans.

Intra-African conflicts

With the approaching end of classical colonialism in Africa, the unifying bond of the decolonization struggle that held most African states together might begin to weaken. There is thus the grave danger that intra-African conflicts may increase. We are already witnessing in many parts of Africa serious border conflicts and rivalries. There will be the temptation for outside powers to meddle in such conflicts and to support one side or the other. For the United States to come out clearly in favor of those who seek to resolve African conflicts in an African context would seem to be the prudent course to follow. This would mean that encouragement should be given to the Organization of African Unity (OAU) to strengthen its capability for peacekeeping and conciliation.

Very recently, we have witnessed the enormous difficulties faced by the OAU in seeking to organize effective peacekeeping forces in Chad. The primary difficulty is related to the lack of adequate financial resources to dispatch and maintain a credible peacekeeping force. African leaders have long wished that the major powers would lend assistance, equipment, and financial resources to give the OAU a meaningful peacekeeping machinery. In the Chad situation there was always a lingering doubt in the minds of many Africans as to whether outside forces were working against the introduction of OAU peacekeeping machinery. The United States can work either through the United Nations or directly with the OAU to assist in the establishment of a viable peacekeeping machinery for the OAU.

It is also of some importance that support be given to the OAU for the establishment of a machinery withi the OAU to resolve intra-African disputes. At the last OAU summit meeting in Freetown, Sierra Leone, proposals were tabled for the establishment of a security council to deal with serious political disputes among African states. While the majority were in favor of proceeding, others expressed caution, and the matter is now being studied by the OAU Secretariat for discussion and decision at the next summit meeting to be held in Kenya. Certainly, it will be in the American interest if the African states can develop an effective regional instrument for the settlement of disputes. The convening of heads of state on an emergency basis to deal with crises, such as the meeting on Libyan involvement in Chad, may not be the most appropriate way to resolve urgent problems.

What priority should the United States give to Africa

Africans are realistic and sophisticated enough to realize that the highest national interest of the United States is to protect its security and, in the first instance, to join with its allies in the Atlantic alliance to protect and maintain its security interests in Europe. Africans realize that for a long time to come the United States will be obliged to recognize the defense of Europe as its highest priority.

It is also recognized by the majority of Africans that even in an era of negotiation (as opposed to confrontation) the United States will pay greater attention to those areas where its security and that of its allies are most directly involved. Already, demands are being made within the United States for more military input aimed at defense of the Persian Gulf area and of the lines of communication necessary for the functioning of Western industrial society. Attempts by either superpower to control Africa's strategic mineral resources, or its territory for strategic purposes, could convert the African continent into an area of confrontation. This would, of course, mean Western foreign policy would have to focus increasingly on Africa in an attempt to deter or contain such perceived threats.

Developments in South Africa may also have a major bearing on whether Africa will have a higher priority in the foreign policy calculations of the United States. As was pointed out earlier, there are bound to be major internal developments in South Africa in the 1980s. Should the United States assist efforts to bring about peaceful change, and should the present South African leadership heed such advice, then the climate might be improved. If, however, revolutionary change should get the upper hand, the United States could be faced with one of the greatest challenges. Clearly, a South Africa hostile to the United States would pose a security problem of very serious dimensions.

Realistically, Africa cannot possibly be the number one priority of the United States as a new administration takes office. But it cannot be ignored. The United States must be able to shift priorities in Africa to cope with unforeseen developments. The United States ought to give first attention to the well-being of the African peoples who, having emerged from colonialism, still live today in poverty and underdevelopment. The challenge for the United States is to formulate political, economic, and social policies to strengthen the hand of those in Africa who seriously desire to improve the general situation for the African people, so that they may live in peace and freedom.

DISCUSSION

U.S. NATIONAL INTERESTS IN AFRICA

The discussion converged upon three themes to which both William
Foltz and James Jonah had alluded: that East-West conflict could be
avoided in Africa; that southern Africa is likely to be the focus
of concern and the highest stake for all parties in the next decade;
and that multilateral economic aid is desperately important for most
countries in Africa.

Jonah emphasized that Africans do not want the superpowers
involved in Africa; further, he believed that the Soviets distrust
African leaders and are not likely to make long-term commitments
to them. The Cubans are different, at least in Angola. Others
pointed out that the Soviets only take advantage of internal African conflicts -- as is the case in both Ethiopia and Angola. It
is in the interest of the Soviet Union to have these conflicts drag
on, thus increasing need and dependency. It is in the interests
of the United States to end them. Foltz remarked upon the greatly
increased Soviet capacity to move arms and equipment (and Cuban
manpower) into Africa, which was not the case in the Congo crisis
of the 1960s; the Soviets were willing and able to supply the help
that both the Angolan and Ethiopian governments desperately wanted.
There was no sustained discussion about the reasons for Soviet
willingness to become involved; is it ideology? or a perceived
opportunity to make trouble? or a desire to push weak regimes
toward a firm Marxist orientation? or hope of denying, in the
future, resources to the United States and Europe? or all of these
in some relatively unsorted mixture? While there was agreement
that it is unfortunate to look at Africa through the lens of East-
West conflict, which does not fundamentally alter African needs and
African dynamics, Foltz believed that the United States should
directly confront the fact that Soviet activities in Africa are in
all instances against our interests in long-term stability and
development.

South Africa in particular, and southern Africa in general,
will require difficult and delicate diplomacy in the next decade.

The United States has relatively little leverage on the conditions of internal change in South Africa, where there is already a significant dependence on skilled African labor (e.g., the South African Army is becoming an integrated institution), but it is clearly in our interest to encourage internal change in a way that does not bring violent revolution. Change must be real enough to prevent radical internal troubles in the neighboring "front-line" states, but not so traumatic as to lead to widespread violence in South Africa. This may not be possible, but it does seem to be in our and most Africans' interests.

The third theme was economic aid -- the importance to Africa of multilateral aid programs. U.S. Representative Fenwick (R-N.Y.) pointed out that aid is the least popular policy among her constituents. Foltz remarked that aid is like preventive maintenance: it is much less costly than having to try to rebuild the whole edifice. No one mentioned the high cost of corruption both in waste and in the loss of perceived legitimacy of African aid recipients. There was disagreement on the intrusions of the World Bank and the IMF into a country's internal affairs. Is this really political (Seaga's rather than Manley's Jamaica)? or is it economic necessity? To increase food production is literally a matter of survival. Can it be done?

Both speakers agreed that Africa is not likely to be high on the agenda of critical items for the United States, and that intra-African realignments and conflicts are as likely to condition developments during the next decade as any outside influence. Neither speaker thought it likely that Africans would deny to the United States minerals or other commodities it wanted as long as the price was right. The most difficult situation for America is that of South Africa, not only because of its wealth, but also because it could, if things went badly, stir deep political division within the United States.

MIDDLE EAST

U.S. NATIONAL INTERESTS IN THE MIDDLE EAST

Steven L. Spiegel

The Woodrow Wilson Center seeks to identify the national interests
of the United States in the Middle East, to ascertain the possible
conflicts among disparate American objectives in the area, to
understand emerging developments in the region and the American role
as new patterns emerge, and to consider the relative significance
of American interests in the Middle East by comparison to other
regions. These problems are not easily addressed and represent
some of the most difficult questions confronting American foreign
policy in this decade. The challenge posed by the Center can only
begin to be addressed by understanding the historical and geopolitical context in which the United States today finds itself in
the Middle East.

The historical and geopolitical context

Although specific Americans have been fascinated with the Middle
East for religious, commercial, diplomatic, and cultural reasons
for decades, only after World War II did the United States begin
to play a prominent role in the area. The new American arrival
on the regional scene was announced by the prominent U.S. position
in the Iran crisis of 1946 and by the British withdrawal from
Greece and Turkey in favor of Washington in early 1947 -- which
led to enunciation of the Truman Doctrine, the most important early
postulation of the American approach to the new confrontation with
the Soviet Union.

However, despite Mr. Truman's dramatic statement to Congress,
key foreign policy attention remained focused elsewhere -- on the
recovery of Europe, the future of Germany, Soviet consolidation
of East Europe, the civil war in China. It is ironic that a crisis
of limited strategic significance -- the dispute over the future
of the British mandate in Palestine -- became fixed in the national
and international consciousness as symbolizing the new American
role in the Middle East. While Britain wrestled with the problem
of Palestine, a fierce debate proceeded in this country. Many

favored a Jewish state in part of the mandate in light of the recent destruction of 6 million Jews in Europe and because of Zionist acceptance of the principle that Palestine could be divided into two states -- each with majority Jewish and Arab populations. Others sought to protect American commercial, cultural, and diplomatic concerns in the Arab world, fearing that the majority Arab populace would be hostile to the United States as a consequence of the establishment of a Jewish state, and that American interests would suffer. While the debate proceeded, a frustrated and inconsistent Truman administration sought to avoid undue involvement.

The very fact of U.S. entanglement, however, suggested the dramatic changes that were rapidly occurring in America's international position. The apparent success of the Truman Doctrine, caused by British withdrawal from Greece and Turkey and widespread differences with the British over their handling of the Palestinian question, intensified suspicion of the colonial powers in the area. Americans of a variety of persuasions (including both supporters and opponents of the creation of the state of Israel) tended to see the British and French in particular as impediments to the achievement of commercial and diplomatic interests. Without them, it was thought, many of the area's problems would be solved. Yet, it was never clear how substituting American for European involvement would resolve the difficulties.

As this attitude toward the Europeans suggests, Americans were generally uninitiated in the folkways and subtleties of the Middle East; therefore, the bitterness and intensity of the debate over the future of Palestine had an especially lasting impact because it was the most visible early American confrontation with the area. Many lessons were drawn from the experience by practitioners, pundits, and scholars dealing with the region. Although often repeated until they became nearly principles of policy, these lessons frequently represented false conclusions drawn from limited interaction with the area, and, at the very least, they often misled policymakers into unsatisfactory positions.

First, it became general practice to see the Middle East as equivalent to the Arab-Israeli theater. This conclusion is especially ironic because the major act of the Truman administration in the area was incorporated by the Truman Doctrine, which dealt with Greece and Turkey, states on the periphery of the region. Certainly, Truman himself never viewed Arab-Israeli matters as central even to his Mideast policy. Yet, after Truman the quiescence of major difficulties vis-a-vis such countries as Iran, Turkey, Afghanistan, and Ethiopia reinforced the perception of the dominance of the Arab-Israeli issue.

Second, policy toward the area is perceived in a context of competing Arab-Israeli interests approaching a "zero-sum game." Thus, American policies that aid individual Arab states are evaluated in the context of possible sacrifices to Israeli security, and improvements in relations between Jerusalem and Washington are assumed to threaten the stability of U.S.-Arab contacts and even the survival of individual Arab leaders. Arab rhetoric and Israeli complaints reinforce these images.

Third, because many think that Truman's decision to recognize Israel was based solely on Jewish pressure and was inconsistent with America's strategic interests, American policy toward the Middle East is frequently seen as motivated by domestic -- largely Jewish -- pressure groups that interfere with the State Department's attempts to conduct American policy in a professional manner. Congressional pressure on behalf of Israel is also often seen as preventing presidents from pursuing "American interests." Related to this perception, American policies toward Israel are often viewed as reactions to sentimental attachments, whereas actions taken in favor of the Arabs are often perceived as consistent with realpolitik. Since Israel was born in emotional circumstances, she is frequently conceived of solely in emotional terms when assessments are made of American interests.

Critical events in the quarter-century after Truman's recognition of Israel acted to reinforce these "lessons." After the shah was easily reestablished on the peacock throne, the impression was strengthened that other than Arab-Israeli problems were relatively simple to solve.

When the Eisenhower administration became convinced that the Soviet Union would soon threaten the area, it concluded that the way to thwart possible advances was to solidify relationships with the Arab states. The equation of the Middle East with the Arab-Israeli dispute led key figures to further conclude that sponsoring an Arab-Israeli settlement was the best means of solidifying the Arab-American relationship.

When the strategy failed, the Suez crisis further reinforced previous lessons, because the Arab-Israeli war coincided with and was identified with a simultaneous alliance crisis and a Soviet-American confrontation. This pattern of overlapping crises was again relived in the Six Day War. By 1969, when President Nixon entered office, he referred to the area as a "powder keg"; the equation of another Arab-Israeli war with a Soviet-American confrontation was set. The experiences of Eisenhower, Johnson, and Nixon seemed to teach that without an Arab-Israeli problem Soviet-American confrontations and alliance crises over the Mideast would not occur.

These collective historical experiences became concretized and embellished as an unquestioned shibboleth in Washington when Egypt and Syria attacked Israel in October 1973. The Yom Kippur War led to the overlapping of another ingredient alongside the usual Arab-Israeli, intra-alliance, and Soviet-American confrontations:

the energy crisis. Given past lessons and the pressure of recent
events, it seemed obvious to policymakers that an Arab-Israeli
settlement would lead to an amelioration, if not elimination, of
the Soviet alliance, would reduce energy challenges the United
States faced, and would prevent future Arab oil embargoes.

Just as this paradigm of American policy toward the area had
become set in Washington, the seeds of its undoing had already been
sown. Although the old postulates had been deceptive and inaccu-
rate, a variety of factors contributed to their apparent applica-
bility. First, they were based on the continuing stability of the
Persian Gulf created by the British presence. Further, they assumed
continuing American influence in such "peripheral" countries as
Iran and Ethiopia. Perhaps most important, they presupposed that
conflict among the Arab states would be controlled because of the
rhetoric of Arab unity and the common adversary of Israel. The
neutrality of poor but strategically located Afghanistan was also
assumed to be a permanent condition of the area.

Gradually, all of these conditions disappeared. First, in
1968 the British announced that they would leave the Persian Gulf
in 1971. The United States decided to replace the British with
Iranian forces. This decision in turn led to condoning oil-price
increases in order to bankroll the shah so that he would be able
to build up his armed might as policeman in the Persian Gulf.
Ultimately, the disruption in Iran caused by the country's newly
found wealth contributed to the regime's disintegration.

Second, although the United States made significant gains in
Egypt, the Sudan, and Somalia in the 1970s, there was a gradual decline in the Anglo-American role in the area, which led to the
emergence of regimes closely aligned with the Soviet Union in both
South Yemen and Ethiopia. Further, the traditional neutrality of
Afghanistan was severed by a Marxist coup in 1978, which led ultimately to the Soviet invasion of December 1979.

Third, oil prices began to increase markedly by 1971, and even
before the October 1973 war it was clear that major price hikes
were imminent. Although a new era of Arab unity seemed to be emerging when prices quadrupled in 1974, the price hikes actually accelerated tensions among competing Arab states. As Arab financial
and commercial importance grew, the long-standing strains within
the Arab world also increased. The pressures were intensified by
the attention riveted on the area by a Western world anxious for
its oil. The result was a heightened series of conflicts within
the region, which served to dissipate the presumed unifying effect
of common antagonism to Israel. These new tensions were further
exacerbated by the Egyptian-Israeli peace treaty and by the emergence of a fundamentalist, anti-Western Shiite regime in Teheran
committed to exporting its particular brand of religious fervor
to its neighbors.

     The first indication of a breakdown of even symbolic unity
after October 1973 occurred when the long-tolerated communal compro-
mise in Lebanon dissolved into full-scale civil war in 1975-76 --
ultimately engaging several outside forces, of which the most complex was Syria. The examples of internecine conflict began to
mount thereafter as tensions developed in such disparate locales
as Saudi Arabia, Iraq, and Syria, and spilled over into non-Arab
Iran and Turkey. Fron the late 1970s onward, examples of conflict
across borders rose between Libya and her neighbors, between Morocco
and the Algerian-backed Polasario over the future of the former
Spanish Sahara, between the Yemens, between Iraq and Syria, between
Jordan and Syria, and finally and most dramatically between Iraq
and Iran. The clearest example that even the pretense of Arab
unity had been shattered was highlighted by Libyan and Syrian
willingness to break ranks and back the Persians against a fellow
Arab country. The most populous Arab country and traditional
leader, Egypt, had, of course, already broken ranks completely by
signing a peace treaty with Israel.

     This plethora of events -- occurring at rapid pace in the late
1970s -- has destroyed the basis for equating America's Middle East
problems with either the Arab-Israeli conflict in general or the
Palestinian question in particular. Of course, old ideas die hard,
and many authorities and officials have understandably been reluctant to part with ideas to which they have grown accustomed.

     By 1980 it was preposterous to argue that settling the future
of the West Bank -- the new code for settling the Arab-Israeli dispute -- could also substantially ameliorate the energy problem,
settle the future of Iran and Afghanistan, ensure the political
stability of the Persian Gulf, or resolve the threat of Soviet encroachments in the area. Indeed, by the late 1970s, it should
have been clear that the 1948-based paradigm had failed to fit
specific facts. Thus:

     1) Despite the apparent link between oil prices and the Pales-
tinian question, and the expectation that future difficulties would
be caused by another Arab oil embargo, the second oil shock in
1979 occurred over a totally unrelated matter -- the upheaval in
Iran. A potential third shock in 1981 could occur over a similar
non-Israeli factor, the Iran-Iraq War.

     2) Despite the supposed link between American treatment of
the Arab states and the future of the Soviet role in the region,
the Kremlin made its initial breakthrough in the area in Egypt in
1955 at a time of American distance from Israel. In turn, it
suffered its greatest reversal (again in Egypt) in 1972 when American relations with Israel were especially close, and with Egypt
particularly distant.

     3) Despite the presumption that pressure on Israel leads to
improved relations with Arab states, and that major amounts of aid to

Israel result in alienation from the Arabs, two of the major historical events of the post-1945 period suggest the exact opposite. At Suez and afterward, the United States pressured Israel, and Washington's regional influence plummeted. In October 1973 the American position was enhanced in some sectors of the Arab world even though Washington bestowed a massive arms airlift upon Jerusalem. What these experiences suggest is that the connection between aid to Israel and relations with the Arab states is far more complex than is usually supposed. In specific circumstances pressure on Israel does not guarantee improved relations with leading Arab states, and aid to Israel does not prevent expanded contacts with pro-American Arab regimes.

4) Despite the supposition that domestic politics determine our Mideast policy, individual presidencies have not substantiated this claim. For example, Jimmy Carter -- with heavy Jewish support -- frequently alienated the Jewish community as a consequence of his Middle East policy. On the other hand, Richard Nixon -- with little Jewish support -- was responsible for dramatic increases in American aid to Israel.

5) Despite the persistent conception that even a partial Arab-Israeli peace would resolve basic American dilemmas in the Middle East, a peace treaty between Israel and the most populous and most important of the Arab countries (long the dream of U.S. policymakers) has not improved our prospects in the area and, viewing the region as a whole, has coincided with a deterioration of American interests.

6) Despite the notion that the bureaucracy is most often able to assess accurately our interests in the area, major misjudgments abound. Thus, before October 1973 it was universally and mistakenly assumed that Israeli strength was sufficient to deter an Arab attack, and Israeli intelligence accurate enough to prevent surprise in the unlikely event that the Arabs would be foolish enough to dare to attack. On the other hand, American policy has always maintained that since no Arab state would accept the objective of normalized peace with Israel in the foreseeable future, it would not be productive for the United States to propound it. Yet, eight months after Carter became the first president to advocate Arab-Israeli normalization, Sadat was in Jerusalem.

7) Despite the confident notion that the sources and producers of petroleum could be controlled, the 1970s are filled with disappointments. Most dramatically, the shah did not prove to be a durable replacement for the British as protector of the Persian Gulf. In the context of price arrangements, the seminal 1971 Teheran oil agreement was supposed to stabilize the international petroleum market, a prediction that had been disproved well before October 1973. The sale of F-15s to Riyadh in 1978 was supposed to lead to the Saudis' increased moderation on the Israel question and a closer relationship with Washington. On both counts Saudi policy has since moved in the opposite direction.

Thus, the shattering events of the late 1970s should have confirmed that presumed American lessons dating back to the Truman
administration had not really functioned as adequate guides for
U.S. conduct in the Middle East. Quite the contrary, generally
accepted postulates often confused policymakers and led them in
directions that ultimately created both shocks and frustrations.
While the complexity of the area defies simple principles upon which
policies might be conducted, misleading assumptions consistently
precipitated faulty contexts in which policies were formulated.

American officials cannot afford to continue to rely on traditional assumptions and approaches toward the area because conditions in the Middle East over the next decade are likely to worsen
rather than improve. Now that the unraveling of the structure of
political relations in the Persian Gulf has begun, it will be
difficult to arrest growing areas of instability let alone to
reverse the process. The period 1978-1980 may serve as an example.
A crisis within Iran was followed by the fall of the shah, which
in turn was followed by growing chaos within Iran, the hostage
crisis, the Mecca incident, the Soviet invasion of Afghanistan,
the Iran-Iraq War. Each of these developments could soon lead to
a series of events that could further destabilize the oil trade
and/or enhance Soviet influence in the region. The dangers
mount.

On the other hand, the peace process between Cairo and Jerusalem does not have as severe a potential negative impact on American interets. By comparison with a decade or even a half-decade
ago, the thrust of Egyptian-Israeli events has been in a positive
direction as epitomized by the disengagement accords in 1974 and
1975, the Sadat visit to Jerusalem, the Camp David accords, the
Egyptian-Israeli peace treaty, the autonomy talks. While most
daily headlines reflect disappointments and frustrations, both
Egypt and Israel are clearly committed to the process, which cannot
be completed until the new administration in Washington has formulated policies of its own and the outcome of the Israeli elections
is known. Even in the unlikely, but conceivable, event that the
entire Egyptian-Israeli peace process were to disintegrate, the
impact on American regional interests -- though decidedly negative --
is not likely to be worse than the consequences of a crumbling
Western position throughout the Persian Gulf -- a far more predictable eventuality in the coming decade. Yet, past assumptions have
led us to anticipate that developments in the Arab-Israeli arena
will be more threatening to our interests.

Determining national interests -- toward a new set of guidelines

Since past assumptions about the area have been unsatisfactory, it
is necessary to seek a new philosophy for dealing with the region.
The first step in this process is to comprehend American national
interests in the area. Fortunately, the Middle East is one region

where there is little disagreement about the identity of these fundamental interests. In other areas, there can be considerable controversy over such an issue. For example, should the approach to the Soviet Union be one of confrontation or detente? Should China policy be based on an alliance against the U.S.S.R., on potential relations with Beijing, or on protecting Taiwan? In the Middle East, by contrast, the objectives of policy are widely accepted:

1) The prevention of Soviet military expansion and the limitation of the number of Soviet clients and radical anti-Western regimes in the area;

2) the concomitant promotion of pro-Western regimes and their stability;

3) the continued flow of oil to the United States, Japan, and Europe;

4) the maintenance of open sea lanes for transporting oil;

5) the limitation of regional conflicts that might impede other U.S. interests in the area, such as the Arab-Israeli dispute, Lebanon, the Iran-Iraq War.

There has been disagreement, however, on how to implement these goals. For example, Eisenhower, in pursuing anti-Soviet objectives, sought to block the Russians by organizing the Arab states, while Nixon, pursuing identical objectives, was prepared to consider Israel an asset. U.S. officials have traditionally argued about how to make inroads in the Arab world. John Foster Dulles favored stressing the role of conservative Iraq, while many critics and operatives in the area believed that Nasser's Egypt should be wooed. A quarter-century later the roles have reversed. Now official American policy favors Sadat's Egypt and many critics believe that radical Iraq should be considered strongly in American concerns. In approaching the question of regional stability, the controversy over Camp David has replaced the American debate about the Eisenhower Doctrine. Similarly, in the 1970s a bitter tactical dispute raged over how to handle the Arab oil producers -- whether to seek wide-ranging agreements or whether to adopt a confrontation strategy, leading perhaps even to seizure of the oil fields. As has become typical of the American experience in the Middle East, in all of these cases there has been no disagreement among disputing Americans over goals, but rather their differences have centered on tactics.

Thus, debate in this country about the Middle East is not about identifying interests, but rather about the best ways of securing these interests. Therefore, what is needed in the American approach to the region is a more accurate set of postulations that would more successfully guide specific policymaking. An attempt to provide several alternatives to the assumptions that have operated in the past follows:

First, the area should be recognized for what it is -- a highly factionalized region divided between peoples and movements of diverse and competing backgrounds, religious interests, and objectives. Even within supposedly united communities (e.g., the Arab world) differences are sharp and conflicts bitter. Therefore, in evaluating its interests the United States cannot afford to isolate one dispute (i.e., between the Arabs and Israel) at the expense of understanding and preparing for problems that may arise as a consequence of other conflicts. As the experience of the late 1970s suggests clearly, to focus almost exclusively on Arab-Israel matters is to ignore a host of other problems potentially more dangerous to U.S. interests in the Middle East.

Second, we must recognize that the new conditions created by increased political interdependence with the entire area mean that our relations with an expanding region are far more intricate and complicated than in the past. A simplistic but often prevailing view is that the need for Arab oil creates diplomatic and economic pressures on the United States, while Israel benefits from an American domestic constituency that U.S. presidents heed.

In today's Middle East, however, the pressures multiply, and they operate in more than one direction. American actions in the Ethiopian-Somali dispute, or in reaction to the Soviet invasion of Afghanistan, or regarding the Iranian hostage crisis, affect attitudes about U.S. policy throughout the Persian Gulf and the Arab-Israeli theater. Relations with oil producers are also becoming more complicated. With a continuing war between Iran and Iraq and emerging tensions between Libya and Nigeria over Qaddafi's evolving thrust into Africa, it is necessary to develop a variety of alternative policies toward the oil producers, with the accompanying realization that in this newly politically interdependent international system these policies will affect our relations with the rest of the area.

Even oil-poor countries such as Egypt and Israel develop leverage in this type of system. The United States has acquired a stake in the success of President Sadat because of his pro-U.S., anti-Soviet regional stance, and because of his reliance on peaceful negotiations -- long a fundamental tenet of American foreign policy. Similarly, independent of domestic politics, it is difficult to pressure Jerusalem because Israel has become a symbol of American credibility due to her traditional, close relationship with the United States, her democratic character, and past American commitments to her. If the United States is not capable of protecting countries closely interdependent with us politically, other governments will include in their calculations revised assessments of U.S. willingness and ability to protect friendly countries.

There is another face to dependence: The Israelis need our arms, our economic aid, and our diplomatic support. The Arab producers need our market, our protection, our goods, and our technical skills. We bankroll the Israelis in the form of aid, the Arab producers in the form of oil payments. Even the Iranians have acknowledged their dependence on us through their variety of specific demands during the prolonged hostage crisis. Any of these parties can have a devastating effect on one aspect of our international security, but at the same time we also can destroy their security by our actions. This intricate mutual dependence means that we must redefine our conception of the area, the problems we confront, and the means of protecting our interests.

Third, we should recognize that the United States is sufficiently powerful and is seen as sufficiently powerful -- to affect the thrust of local developments in the region. Those who seek to decrease the use of American power in the hopes of diminishing the image of the United States as a colonial power are likely to be disappointed when the United States is still seen in imperialist terms. Since the countries of the area expect the United States to be strong, weakness does not result in improved relations because the new behavior is not compatible with their image of America, and because a weak America is less useful to friendly regimes and less important to the region. Thus, U.S. forbearance toward the new government in Iran did not avert the hostage crisis. Repeated efforts to accommodate Arab oil producers have not prevented constantly rising prices. Carter administration overtures at various times to the PLO, Syria, Iraq, and Libya did not moderate their policies any more than Eisenhower's and Kennedy's approaches to Nasser moderated his.

The challenge for U.S. policy in the area is not to work toward eliminating the appearance of imperialism, which is in any case only in the eye of the beholder, and it is not to appear reasonable to individual states. Rather, the challenge is to mobilize support from individual regimes, to protect leaders who have become identified as allies of Washington, and to demonstrate that we possess a mixture of political and military power (actual and symbolic) that can be translated into a recipe for stemming the tide of regional instability and volatility.

Fourth, in the Middle East signals are especially important, and when American administrations create an impression of vacillation -- even unintentionally -- the consequences are devastating. For example, the Eisenhower administration wavered toward Egypt between offers of largesse (arms, the Aswan Dam) and acts of confrontation (Aswan renege, Eisenhower Doctrine) with disastrous results. On the other hand, by the middle of the Nixon era it was clear that U.S. leaders were determined to protect Israel from being attacked, but not to assist her in any offensive strategy; they would work with Arab states, but not to aid Soviet clients. Whatever its strengths or weaknesses, this policy was clearer than policy during the Eisenhower or Carter eras, when there was continued confusion in the Middle East concerning the identity of specific U.S. policy aims vis-a-vis Israel, Iran, the radical Arabs, and even the U.S.S.R.

Because of increased political and economic interdependence with the Middle East, consistency is essential, especially given the increased American concentration on the area. An inconsistent policy undermines the exercise of American power that the United States seeks to project. At the same time it causes the states of the region to become seriously confused over the rules of behavior the United States considers acceptable.

Fifth, we must recognize that the central energy problem of our Mideast policy is assuring adequate supplies of petroleum from the area, rather than manipulating price. The price of oil relates to questions of regulating the international economy, which are by no means connected exclusively to the Middle East. Even if this area were as tranquil as Europe, and none of the major conflicts were occurring, the problems of dealing with high oil prices and handling petro-billions would remain.

Under current conditions the security of oil supplies could be threatened by any of a number of developments -- including a blocking of the critical sea lanes; Soviet incursion into the Persian Gulf; revolution or upheaval in a major petroleum exporter, especially Saudi Arabia; regional wars in the Persian Gulf, such as an expansion of the conflict between Iran and Iraq; or even by another Arab-Israeli war. Therefore, the task of our Mideast policy is to focus on developing the means for preventing all of these contingencies from arising since any one of them could have serious consequences for the Western economies.

Sixth, we must recognize that it is essential in an area as volatile as the Mideast to establish a clear vision of what the United States seeks to accomplish, and to communicate that vision unambiguously to all of the states of the area. We must also convey the means we will use to effect our strategy and the instruments that are available and therefore credible. Otherwise, any vision presented will not be believed or supported by the states of the area.

In projecting the vision it is an error to rank interests, since American concerns in this region are interlinked and cannot be separated. For example, we must recognize that as American involvement in the Middle East has intensified, the means by which the U.S.S.R. could threaten U.S. interests have also expanded (e.g., Soviet involvement in areas previously peripheral to Mideast politics, such as Afghanistan, Ethiopia, South Yemen, and Libya). Soviet advances could threaten access to the oil fields, regional stability, open sea lanes, Israeli security, or the survival of pro-Western regimes. The least likely but most lethal form of Soviet

involvement would be an actual invasion, but past experience has
amply demonstrated that subversion or overt programs for improving
relations with specific regimes can also cause considerable damage
to Western interests. On the other hand, anti-Western movements
indigenous and authentic to the country of origin can have as great
if not a greater negative impact on American interests, as Khomeini's
Iran illustrates. Similarly, an upheaval in the Persian Gulf --
especially in Saudi Arabia -- or a blockade of the Strait of Hormuz
would have an immediate and devastating impact on the economies of
the West.

A vision is only effective if it applies to the problems of the
region as a whole. The inclination to argue that U.S. problems in
the area are a consequence of our support for Israel is an example
of a prominent tendency in U.S. foreign policy to isolate individual
issues while pretending others do not exist. It may be true that
American relations with specific states at particular times (e.g.,
Egypt in 1970, but not in 1980; Jordan in 1980, but not in 1970)
might have been eased if Israel did not represent a competing force
for American support or largesse. Yet, American problems in the
area would also be eased if there were no oil underground and
if the Soviet Union were in a more distant location. Any attempt
to hypothesize about what the area might be like if one of its
essential elements had never existed is irrelevant to present concerns: all of these forces do occur simultaneously. The pitfalls
of this type of approach were demonstrated when the Carter administration presented a vision for dealing with the Arab-Israeli issue
-- only to confront multiple crises elsewhere in the region.

Conclusion

This adjustment to a new set of guidelines is especially crucial
because of the global significance the Middle East has assumed.
The area has become central both in terms of the competition with
the U.S.S.R. and with respect to the West's energy resources. Moreover, because the European allies and Japan depend so heavily on
Mideastern oil, they have come to measure their relationship with
the United States in part by its effectiveness in dealing with the
interconnected problems of the area. When U.S. failures have
occurred, the allies have responded by embracing detente no matter
what actions the U.S.S.R. has taken elsewhere and by acquiescing
to verbal Arab demands as a means of satisfying their immediate
needs.

The Middle East has become a focus of American international
concern even though it is not as close as Central America; even
though individual countries are not as important in terms of com-
patibility of values as the West Europeans or the Japanese (Israel
is an exception); and even though no country in the area possesses
the worldwide strategic significance of Japan, China, France,
Great Britain, or West Germany. It is the very instability and

volatility of the region, when combined with its location and the crucial resources it contains, that make it today the focal point of world politics. The United States is therefore likely to be judged by friend and foe alike by its performance in this crucial area.

This country cannot succeed, however, if it continues to adopt lessons learned and assimilated in earlier and easier times when it could afford to isolate one set of problems and apply them to all events throughout the region. Only a restructuring of the way we perceive the Middle East will make it possible to confront effectively this critical challenge of the 1980s: the challenge to develop policies to protect our diverse but interconnected concerns throughout this region.

U.S. NATIONAL INTERESTS IN THE MIDDLE EAST:
A NEW APPROACH FOR THE 1980s

Les Janka

Short of preventing nuclear war, there is no higher priority for
U.S. policymakers than ensuring the peace, stability, and independence of the Middle East and Persian Gulf region. Trends in
the area -- and our failures of perception and policy -- have vastly
complicated this task. Yet our stake in the region is so vital
that failure in this pursuit could jeopardize the economic health
of the West and Japan, the prestige and credibility of the United
States as a world leader, the cohesion of the Western alliance,
and the global balance of power.

    Our fundamental national interests in the region fall into
four categories: maintaining freedom of access to oil, preventing
the expansion of Soviet power and influence in the area, developing our economic and political cooperation with the Arab world,
and honoring our commitment to the independence and security of
Israel.

    The challenge lies not in identifying these interests, but in
developing an approach to the region that enables us simultaneously
to pursue such diverse and sometimes competing objectives. The
first step is to assess our priorities among these interests and
within our fundamental global interests.

    In the Middle East the top American priority is, and must be,
assured access to the region's oil supplies. Although we may wish
it otherwise, the United States is critically dependent on Middle
Eastern oil to meet domestic energy needs and to support the economic survival of Western Europe and Japan, whose collapse would
radically alter our own political and economic future as well as
the global strategic environment. We currently rely on the region
for 30 percent of our oil imports. The statistics for our allies
are even more dramatic: 67 percent for Western Europe and 75 percent for Japan. Even with massive efforts to conserve and to
develop alternate sources, there is simply no prospect that the
West and Japan will be able to free themselves from this dependency
in the near term.

The realities of our global competition with the Soviet Union, combined with our need for Middle Eastern oil, require that we also place an equally high priority on limiting Soviet influence in the area. The greatest threat from a significantly expanded Soviet influence in the Middle East is not that Moscow would directly cut off Western oil supplies, although projected Soviet energy problems indicate that the Soviets might wish to divert a share of Middle Eastern production for their own use or that of Eastern Europe. The greatest danger is that, in acquiring a dominant influence in the oil-producing countries, the Soviet Union would gain unparalleled economic and political leverage, forcing the West Europeans and Japanese to accommodate themselves to Soviet power and shifting the global balance virtually overnight.

Close behind the above two priorities is a major interest in maintaining our commitment to the security and independence of Israel. This is essential to our own ideals and to our international credibility; it is crucial to insuring domestic support for our foreign policy; and it is a sine qua non of peace in the Middle East. If the dispossession of the Palestinians has created instability, we should not imagine that a genuine threat to Israel's existence would do less. Moreover, our unquestionable commitment to Israel's security is essential if we are to play a mediating role in the Middle East, an element regarded as crucial by the Arab states, which believe Israel will not deal with them directly. For all these reasons, the United States cannot afford to leave any doubt about its commitment to Israel's survival and independence.

Finally, the United States has broad and general interests in continuing and expanding its cooperation with the Arab world. This is key to maintaining the stability of the international financial system, managing the flow of energy supplies, building markets for our goods, and maintaining military and commercial communication throughout the region.

If, in a global context, a restoration of American military credibility abroad and the recovery of our economy at home are the priority objectives of a new administration anxious to restore the U.S.-Soviet balance, then continued access to Middle East oil is necessary to make the first two possible. Fitting this objective into the larger framework of U.S. ends and means drives the priorities and trade-offs that must be made (but are often overlooked) in the Middle Eastern theater. In such a global perspective, the traditional U.S. support for Israel must be secondary to secure energy supplies. As contrary to established Washington rhetoric and domestic political pressures as this might be, such an unfettered view will ultimately serve Israel's interests as well. Not only is Israel's ultimate security directly dependent upon U.S. military and economic strength, but only such a perspective on U.S. interests will produce a set of Middle East policies capable of bringing peace to Israel and stability to the entire region.

132

What the future holds and requires

In selecting the best means for securing American interests in the
Middle East it is essential to look as well at some of the other
dynamics that will shape the area in the coming decade. Within the
region we can expect to see (1) a continuation of the destabilizing
effects of the Arab-Israeli conflict, (2) new challenges to the internal stability of Arab states resulting from rapid economic and
social transformation, and (3) divisions and rivalry within the
Arab world, with the potential for additional regional conflict
among Arab states or between Arabs and Iran. Coinciding with these
trends is a renewed energy in the historic Soviet drive for influence in the region -- reflected in the Soviet-Syrian friendship
treaty, the perceptible Soviet "tilt" toward Iran, President Brezhnev's call for a great-power agreement neutralizing the Persian
Gulf -- and, witness Afghanistan, greater Soviet capability and
readiness to project military forces beyond Soviet borders.

If the United States is to have a rational approach that meets
the challenges of the 1980s and secures American interests in this
complex environment, we must take a fresh, hardheaded look at our
recent Middle East policies and at the basic policy assumptions
that lie behind them. The current combination of crises and stalemate gives the new administration an excellent opportunity to begin
this process. But it must start by removing traditional blinders
created by certain "myths" that have narrowed the American vision
of the Middle East. This paper is an effort to put aside the tena-
cious rhetoric that confuses this issue and to lay out another
approach to the problem, including some thoughts not often discussed in Washington.

American-Israeli relations

The first cluster of "myths" that stands in the way of a rational
Middle East policy centers on the emotional question of our rela-
tionship with Israel. It includes the assumptions (1) that Ameri-
can interests in the Middle East coincide precisely with those of
Israel, (2) that Israel is a significant stategic asset to the
United States, and (3) that time is on Israel's side.

(1) Identity of Interests   While we cannot tolerate a challenge
to Israel's survival, we must recognize that U.S. interests extend
beyond that issue and that our Israeli friends are not the only
actors in the region. There are 150 million Arabs whose aspirations and actions critically affect vital American interests.

Largely due to domestic political considerations, American
leaders have consistently failed to distinguish between the American
commitment to the security of Israel and Washington's acceptance of
and support for the particular views and policies of a given Israeli
government. Our support for Israel need not be unquestioning or

unlimited, but too often it has led us to surrender our own independence of perception and policy in the Middle East. Our relations
with the Arab world are badly served by the impression we have given
that the Israeli government has a veto over American policies. The
Carter administration's decision to disavow, under strong Israeli
and domestic pressures, its March 1980 U.N. vote condemning Israeli
settlements in occupied territory -- settlements the administration
had consistently characterized as illegal -- is a humiliating case
in point.

(2) Strategic Asset   The basis for the U.S. commitment to Israel's survival is not fundamentally strategic. We must distinguish
Israel's need to be important to the United States from our real
strategic imperatives. Israel does not have a major function in
the traditional East-West military calculus, and Pentagon contingency
planning does not rely on more than a tertiary Israeli contribution
to the West's strategic position. Indeed, Israel most frequently
enters contingency planning out of concern that a new war between
Israel and its Arab neighbors might be the spark that provokes a
broader war between the superpowers.

Israeli leaders insist that their country is a major democratic
bulwark against the spread of Soviet influence in the region -- a
claim based in part on the fact that the Arab armies Israel fought
in 1967 and 1973 were Soviet armed. A stronger argument can be
made that the polarization of the region resulting from the Arab-
Israeli conflict and the Arab search for arms has been the major
source of Soviet opportunities. Communism and the Soviet system
have generally held little attraction for Moslem societies.

Israel's respected military capability and superb facilities
are indeed valuable potential assets to the United States, but their
actual utility is highly dependent upon the nature of the crisis in
which we might need them. As we develop new approaches to security
in the region, we must recognize that as long as Israel holds onto
the occupied territories, our Arab allies will find military cooperation that involves Israel unacceptable and destablilizing. What
is more, the prolongation of the Arab-Israeli conflict and our
close support for, and consequent identification with, Israel will
continue to severely limit our own ability to forge closer security
links with Arab states aimed at restricting Soviet influence.

(3) Time   It is true that the peace treaty with Egypt has neu-
tralized the threat to Israel's western front and shifted the military balance. Yet Israel's occupation of the West Bank and Gaza
Strip and the continued state of no-war-no-peace with the rest of
the Arab world is creating political, demographic, economic, and
military pressures that Israel cannot sustain indefinitely.

Continued control of the West Bank and Gaza will alter the
character of Israel itself, a prospect that already deeply dis-
turbs many Israelis. Protracted military occupation, based on

coercion rather than consent, will distort the concept of Israeli democracy, weaken the morale of the Israeli military, and divide Israeli society. Yet the alternative of annexing the West Bank and Gaza with their 1.2 million Arab inhabitants poses an even greater dilemma. Given present demographic trends, Arabs will soon constitute close to half the Israeli population, forcing the government either to alter the fundamental definition of Israel as a Jewish state or to disenfranchise (or expel) a large segment of its inhabitants.

In addition, the defense burden required to maintain the status quo is straining the already shaky Israeli economy. Military expenditures now equal 40 percent of Israel's GNP, a fourfold increase over 1966 (evidence that expanded borders have not brought security). This extraordinary level of defense spending is sustainable only at the price of growing dependence on U.S. aid and distortions of the Israeli production base.

Yet Israel cannot rely on the United States to provide an indefinite subsidy, particularly in support of policies that are widely viewed as standing in the way of peace. The rejection last year of Israel's request for an extra $1.6 billion in aid on top of an annual $1.7 billion aid package stunned many Israelis into recognizing that U.S. financial assistance may not be unlimited. To the degree that acts of political repression on the West Bank undermine the image of Israeli democracy, and divisiveness in the Israeli body politic increases, American support for a "stable and democratic ally" will be increasingly open to challenge. More ominously, there is the real possibility that future Arab oil embargoes -- if related to Israeli intransigence -- may provoke an anti-Jewish backlash in the American body politic.

In short, the United States is doing neither itself nor Israel a favor by allowing Israeli intransigence and preference for the status quo to set the pace for American policy.

American-Palestinian relations

A second major cluster of "myths" standing in the way of a rational American policy in the region centers on the issue of the Palestinians. Included are the assumptions (1) that we should avoid recognizing the Palestinian right to self-determination, (2) that we should not talk to the Palestine Liberation Organization, and (3) that a Palestinian state is unacceptable.

(1) Self-determination   The moral values of our own society, as well as our pragmatic interests in the Middle East, require that the United States recognize the reality of Palestinian nationalism and the right of the Palestinian people to self-determination.

We may be unable, as we were at Camp David, to persuade Israel
to recognize this right -- just as we are unable to persuade the
PLO to begin by recognizing Israel's existence. But that should
not prevent us from articulating an American position based on our
own values and perceptions. The formula put forward by the Carter
administration -- that the Palestinians have a right to "participate" in the determination of their own future -- is inadequate.
It satisfied neither our historical commitment to the principle of
self-determination nor the national aspirations of the Palestinians -- witness their refusal to participate in the Camp David
autonomy talks.

Our unwillingness to recognize a Palestinian right to self-
determination has a number of costs. It puts us at odds with our
major European allies. It drives a wedge between us and friendly
Arab governments and makes it politically impossible for them to
join an American peace process. (Our insensitivity to this fact
has led us to apply abrasive diplomatic pressure on the Saudis and
others in hopes of winning their support for Camp David, only to
find that we are forcing them to distance themselves further from
us.) And, perhaps most importantly, it has enabled us to sidestep
the heart of the Middle East problem, which is no longer the negotiation of agreements between Israel and her Arab neighbors, but a
reconciliation of the Palestinians' right to self-determination
with Israel's right to independence and security.

Moreover, there is no validity to a pervasive "sub-myth" that
most Arab leaders really do not want to see the emergence of a Palestinian entity. Former Ambassador Robert Neumann cogently reflected
a more accurate Arab view:

> Yes, the Saudis are acutely sensitive to the Soviet threat
> but they realize also that they and other Arab states are par-
> ticularly vulnerable to that threat because of their instabil-
> ity. And the most pervasive threat to their stability comes
> from the still unresolved Palestinian question. One million
> Palestinians are estimated to live and work in Saudi Arabia
> and the Gulf States....If those Palestinians came to believe,
> once again, that their interests had been slighted, and espe-
> cially if they concluded that their host countries had taken
> part in or tolerated this "conspiracy," they could become a
> dangerous source of instability. Certainly the tragedy of
> Lebanon, although a separate and most complex case, illus-
> trates on a daily basis to what extent enraged Palestinians
> can destabilize a country.[1]

---

[1] Washington Quarterly, Spring 1979, p. 32.

(2) _Dialogue_   The Palestinians are the central issue in establishing peace between Israel and the Arab world. Palestinian nationalism is a living reality that cannot be defined away. Whether we
approve of the fact or not, the PLO is the only spokesman the Palestinians have. If we want to talk to the Palestinians, we must talk
to the PLO -- a fact vividly demonstrated by the complete failure
of the Camp David process to bring forth an alternative set of
West Bank leaders with whom to negotiate.

Ambassador Neumann again makes an important historical point:

It should be clear that no Palestinian settlement can have
much reality without participation of the Palestinians themselves. This seemingly obvious rule of common human logic
has always been strenuously opposed by those who controlled
people and territories that they were unwilling to give up
...In Algeria the French refused for a long time to consider the National Front of Liberation (FLN) as valid negotiating partners claiming that they did not really represent the population. The British tried the same in Cyprus.
The United States had a similar attitude toward the Viet-
cong during the Vietnamese war.

But if peace, real peace, were to be established in any of
those areas, reality had, at long last, to be faced. If
one wants peace, one has to talk with the people who carry
guns.[2]

The fact that Israel will not now talk to the PLO does not
require us to surrender our own freedom of diplomatic action in an
area that is vital to our interests. Indeed, Israel's inability
to begin the negotiating process makes the U.S. role all the more
urgent. But how can repeated American assertions that the Palestinians are the "heart of the problem" have any credibility when
no U.S. official can talk to their representatives?

The sticking point has been the PLO's refusal to support
explicitly U.N. Resolution 242 and to recognize Israel's right to
exist. Henry Kissinger promised Israeli leaders in 1975, as part
of the eleventh hour drive to secure Israeli support for the second Sinai disengagement agreement, that we would not recognize or
negotiate with the PLO so long as it did not meet those two conditions. Jimmy Carter unnecessarily compounded the problem by
reiterating that pledge.

The new administration does not have to undermine U.S. credibility by rejecting this commitment, but it should not make the
mistake of actively reiterating or placing a renewed emphasis on

---

[2]_Washington Quarterly_, Spring 1979, p. 34.

this stance, nor should it allow a "no recognition" position to
become one of no dialogue at all. Instead, it should recognize
that the PLO has significantly moderated its actual position since
1973 and now appears prepared -- admittedly with some wobbling --
to recognize Israel within approximately its 1967 borders in exchange for a Palestinian government in the West Bank and Gaza
Strip. In one of the clearest indications of this position, PLO
Chairman Yasser Arafat told U.S. Representative Paul Findley (R-Ill.)
in late 1978:

> The PLO will accept an independent Palestinian state con-
> sisting of the West Bank and Gaza with a connecting corri-
> dor and in that circumstance will renounce any and all
> violent means to enlarge the territory of that state. I
> would reserve the right, of course, to use non-violent means,
> that is to say diplomatic and democratic means, to bring
> about the eventual unity of Palestine.

American policy should not be to perpetuate the impasse between Israel and the PLO, but to encourage, through informal but
serious contacts with a broad range of Palestinian representatives,
the real possibilities for overcoming it.

(3) _Palestinian State_   The United States should not reject in
principle the formation of a Palestinian state. Whatever protesta-
tions Israelis, from their tragic national experience, may make,
the United States has no reason to accept uncritically the assertions that such a state would automatically be pro-Soviet, a
terrorist base, or a military threat to Israel. A fledgling Palestinian government would more likely be largely occupied with
developing an economy, building political institutions, and dealing
with refugees. Its emergence through negotiations would certainly
involve substantal pledges of economic support from the West and
from conservative Arab governments like Saudi Arabia. It would
be suicidal for Palestinian leaders to jeopardize this backing --
and the existence of the new state itself -- by allowing the
Soviets to turn the West Bank into a base of operations.

The formation of a Palestinian state through the process of
negotiations also offers Israel and the United States a unique
opportunity to lay the ground rules for the establishment of this
new entity. These would include practical steps to insure Israel's security, such as demilitarized border zones, restrictions
on the arms possessed by the Palestinian state, formal obliga-
tions on the part of the new state to renounce and suppress terrorism, and technical arrangements for surveillance to protect
Israel against surprise attack. The Austrian State Treaty offers
a precedent of imposed neutrality and arms control. These measures could also be supplemented by a U.S.-Israeli defense treaty,
which would almost certainly be part of any final settlement.
The principal constraint on the new state, however, would be its

own vulnerability and the overwhelming military power of Israel, whose territory would virtually surround it.

As for terrorism, there is no reason to assume that, because Palestinian terrorists now carry out raids against Israel, a new Palestinian state would adopt terrorism as a national instrument. It is essential to recognize terrorism for what it is -- the product of particular historical and social conditions, the methods of desperation, and not the attribute of a particular ethnic or religious group. This is as true of the Palestinians as it was of the Israelis in their battle to establish the Jewish state. If we are truly concerned about terrorism and violence in the Middle East, we will have to look not only at the bombs planted in Israeli markets, but at the devastation wrought by Israel in Lebanon. Terrorism has been a constant feature of the conflict between Israelis and Arabs. The only hope for abolishing it lies in altering the historical context, which means the establishment of some kind of Palestinian homeland while at the same time guaranteeing Israel's long-term security.

In fact, a Palestinian state could well be a stabilizing influence. It would give all Palestinians -- whether or not they returned to live in the new state -- a stake in the security and stability of the Middle East. Without a national homeland, the Palestinians will continue to constitute a military and demographic threat both to Israel and to its neighbors. They will remain a potential source of instability and hostility toward the West within the conservative Persian Gulf states. As former Ambassador Hermann Eilts recently noted:

> One might wish otherwise, but the Palestinian problem, unless steps are taken to grapple with its core element, i.e., the refugees, carries the seeds of further deterioration in the Middle East area, including in the Gulf.... An equitable solution to the Palestinian problem, one satisfactory not only to Israel, but also to the Palestinians, is essential if a political climate favorable to continued Western access to Gulf oil and optimum production levels is to be fostered in the years ahead.
>
> The United States itself might ponder whether its interests are likely to be furthered through the permanent resettlement and enfranchisement in the Gulf states of a totally embittered, anti-American Palestinian community.[3]

---

[3]International Security, Fall 1980, p. 86.

A "Pax-Americana" for the Persian Gulf?

A third and final cluster of "myths" and assumptions revolves
around the Soviet threat and the U.S. military presence required
to protect American interests in the region. It includes the
assumptions (1) that the Soviets have overwhelming capabilities
in the region, (2) that Soviet encroachment, rather than local
instability, is the primary threat, and (3) that the U.S. position
will be enhanced by permanent military bases with full-time U.S.
ground forces in the area.

(1) The Soviets   We must be cautious not to accept at face
value the assumption that the Soviets stand ten feet tall on the
borders of the region and that only a substantial U.S. military
presence (in lieu of a Rapid Deployment Force) will suffice to
protect our interests. What is needed is careful, critical analysis, not overreaction.

Despite considerable publicity given to a perceived overwhelming Soviet superiority backed up by 10, 20, or 30 Soviet divisions on its southern borders, a detailed study of the Soviet ability to project that force 1,000 miles toward the Persian Gulf
leads to a somewhat less hysterical view. The Soviet threat is
real, but in terms of an ability either to push heavy armor divisions through the Caucasus and Zagros mountains or to airlift a
division to the Persian Gulf and support it with a well-defended
logistics tail, the Soviet capability is more limited. In short,
their RDF may not be much better than our RDF.

And while it is true that the revolution in Iran seriously
weakened America's strategic position in the region, the trend of
events following Iraq's invasion of Iran shows some remarkable
improvements. Two years ago, who would have predicted the current
presence of a two-carrier task force in the Arabian Sea with 1,800
U.S. Marines aboard, or a U.S. guided missile cruiser (coordinated
by locally based AWACS patrols) providing a significant air defense
barrier at the head of the Persian Gulf?

(2) Internal stability   We must recognize that the major
threats to U.S. security interests in the Persian Gulf are political
and regional in nature rather than direct or indirect Soviet aggression. A U.S. overreaction to such Soviet threats, and a concerted
effort to force our friends in the Persian Gulf to accept that
perception, could in fact exacerbate the regional tensions that
more directly threaten our interests.

While U.S. military capabilities are essential to protect the
Middle East and Persian Gulf from extra-regional and possible
proxy forces, no U.S. military power can provide internal stability.
Our objective should be portrayed and explained to our Arab friends
as a partnership in which we provide deterrence and defense against
mutual external threats, while encouraging our friends to defend

themselves against dangers internal to the region. One urgent requirement, for example, would be strengthening vulnerable oil facilities against sabotage.

(3) <u>Permanent bases</u> We must become sensitive to the fact that too visible an American military presence will contribute to precisely the regional instability we are seeking to avoid. In particular, we should not try to force the acceptance of permanent military bases with full-time U.S. ground forces in the region (we should stop talking about them too). We cannot afford to ignore historic Arab sensitivities to Western encroachment and the sincere warnings from Arab governments with close ties to the West that they cannot accept permanent military bases on their soil. Too many articles have appeared recently that ignore these sensitivities and take for granted the Arab ability to receive a Western presence -- or worse, imply that such bases are aimed at unstable or unfriendly local regimes, rather than at mutual threats.

It is difficult to think of a more counterproductive move on the part of the United States than trying to pressure governments like those of Egypt or Saudi Arabia into providing bases they are convinced will destabilize their own countries. President Sadat, who has taken enormous risks in casting his lot with the United States, has warned that he will tell the new administration to "go to hell" if it tries to pressure him into accepting U.S. military bases on Egyptian soil, especially in a newly recovered Sinai peninsula.

What is needed is an effective American rapid response capability based on an over-the-horizon presence that includes a permanent naval force in the Indian Ocean, access to local facilities in times of crisis, improvement of intelligence and warning capabilities, and pre-positioning of supplies. This must be done in the context of a global restoration of U.S. military capabilities, which will be the real strength underlying any American deterrent in the Persian Gulf.

At the same time we can support indigenous efforts at regional security cooperation and enhance the ability of our friends to defend themselves against local and internal threats. This can be accomplished in part through limited arms sales and military training, along with steps to help regional states improve their own internal security systems against terrorism and local insurgencies.

The bottom line is that we have to reject both the approach that holds that solving the Palestinian problem is a substitute for taking concrete steps to improve our own and our friends' military capability in the Persian Gulf and the approach that offers a purely military response in the belief that stability can be assured without a solution to the Israeli-Palestinian problem.

Conclusion

The new administration will soon be undertaking a major review of
U.S. interests and policies in the Middle East and Persian Gulf.
Given the realities suggested already, the following measures
might be considered in laying a foundation for a new policy based
solidly on the advancement of American interests in the region.

On the Arab-Israeli conflict:

Recognize that the campaign is over and serious work is to
begin; drop the rhetoric and flawed assumptions adopted from
domestic policies.

Keep all options open. Neither reiterate nor reject Kissinger's policy of not recognizing the PLO, but indicate
instead an acceptance of the centrality of Palestinian interests and the need for a dialogue with the Palestinians.

Explore the possibility of working with all parties to
amend (or replace) U.N. Resolution 242 to remove the stigma
of "refugee" status from the Palestinians. This can be
done without altering the basic peace-for-land bargain
contained in the resolution.

Insist, quietly but credibly, that Israel suspend further
settlement activity in the West Bank and Gaza and further
efforts to alter the status of Jerusalem.

Communicate clearly to the Arab side that the United States
will not back away from its commitment to Israel's security
and independence, while making clear that the United States
will not act to protect all of its interests by an approach
that puts it behind all sides' need for a just settlement.

Avoid enchantment with simplistic "Jordanian options," which
expect more of King Hussein than he can deliver (or even
wants) and which could lead to greater instability by over-
looking the reality of a genuine Jordanian nationalism on
the East Bank.

Prepare the American public for an offer of a full defense
treaty with Israel as the capstone of a final settlement, in
lieu of an increasing buildup of Israeli military forces.

Regarding the Persian Gulf and the U.S. military capabilities:

Move in all possible ways to restore our relations with
Saudi Arabia.

Initiate a major study of the security needs of our friends
in the region to determine the most effective way of helping
them defend their own societies against local threats and insurgencies.

Firm up agreements for pre-positioning military supplies in
the region and gaining access for forward operating bases close
to danger areas.

Reorient the RDF to station a major part of it in Europe,
perhaps in Italy. If the United States is to protect Western
interests in the Persian Gulf, our European allies will have
to accept the fact that elements of U.S. forces and equipment
in NATO may have to move to the Middle East. This will effectively reduce the distance disparity between the Americans and
the Soviets in projecting force into the region.

Such a list is obviously not a new "peace plan." It is offered
rather as the beginning point of a new American approach to the
Middle East incorporating more independence in our foreign policy
and more candor in our domestic policies.

DISCUSSION

U.S. NATIONAL INTERESTS IN THE MIDDLE EAST

Les Janka and Steven Spiegel were in almost complete agreement on
the nature of U.S. national interests in the Middle East, but
disagreed sharply both on the ranking of these interests and on
the implementation of policy. American goals in the region, they
agreed, include maintaining access to oil, curbing Soviet expansion
and influence, preventing the rise of radical anti-Western regimes,
ameliorating local conflicts and internal disturbances, and increasing American economic and political influence in the Arab world.
Janka noted that the United States also was committed to the independence and security of Israel.

The speakers differed considerably on the context and nature
of U.S. decision making and on the prospects for attaining American
goals in the region. Spiegel felt that most American analyses of
Mideastern problems, including Janka's, focus too narrowly on the
Arab-Israeli issue, with the consequence that many Americans believe
that the Soviet threat and the energy crisis would virtually
disappear upon settlement of the Palestinian issue. U.S. policy
on the Arab issue, Spiegel maintained, is too often understood in
terms of a "zero-sum game"; helping one side appears to threaten
the other. A third element of this false paradigm, Spiegel stated,
is the perception that domestic (especially Jewish) pressure seriously constrains the conduct of policy. Spiegel felt that events
since the early 1970s -- the energy crisis, Iran and Afghanistan,
and instability in the Persian Gulf -- have demonstrated the bank-
ruptcy of constructing American policy in such a way that a resolution of the Arab-Israeli conflict must take precedence over all
other issues. Instead, the United States should concentrate its
efforts upon other issues, such as oil, the Soviet threat, and
Islamic radicalism.

Janka's analysis differed from Spiegel's in at least three
respects. First, Janka felt that resolving the Arab-Israeli problem constitutes a first and essential step, if not the ultimate
solution, in the achievement of American goals in the Middle East.

Discussants later emphasized that focus on this one issue meant
that Janka was generally more optimistic than Spiegel on the prospects for an eventual comprehensive settlement of Mideastern problems. Second, Janka, a former policymaker, was more willing
than Spiegel to accept compromises and partial solutions as steps
toward a resolution of problems in the Middle East. Third, Janka
was openly critical of the American tendency to put Israel's interests in the Middle East before those of the United States in the
making of policy. Finally, Janka criticized those friends of
Israel who have imposed what he called a degree of one-sidedness
upon the media and upon the expression of U.S. government policy
by engaging in vendettas against individuals who have questioned
some policies of the current Israeli government. It does not serve
the interest of either the United States or Israel, Janka contended,
for Americans to be inhibited from criticizing Israeli policies
when they believe these are unsound in the long run.

Participants in the discussion observed that the Arab-Israeli
conflict is just one of many that can touch off conflagration in
the Middle East; a Palestinian state, then, would not assure
stable oil supplies for the West. But unless some way is found
to enlist moderate Palestinians in the peace process, many felt
no settlement would last long.

Participants offered a wide variety of concrete policy recommendations. Some favored pressure on Israel on the issue of Palestinian statehood and a much-enlarged American military presence
in the Persian Gulf in conjunction with our European allies. The
inability of the United States to enlist coordinated European and
Japanese support in the Persian Gulf was noted as one of the most
disturbing failures of recent American diplomacy. Others questioned
whether the United States has sufficient resources to control events
in the Middle East. Can U.S. policy in the Middle East be defined
when we are unable to determine Soviet intentions? Although a
recent statement by Brezhenev in India indicates that the Soviets
may have an interest in Mideastern stability and an antipathy
toward the radical Muslims, it is not clear what lesson, if any, can
be drawn from Iran. Ought not the United States avoid any obvious
presence that could suggest, in either Egypt or Saudi Arabia, for
example, a "client state" arrangement?

EUROPE

EUROPE IN THE NEXT TEN YEARS: BEYOND PARITY, BEYOND DETENTE

Thomas O. Enders

1

Let me start, as you suggest, with the basic interests.

The central political fact of Europe in this century is that
without the United States there is only one great power present on
the continent. And without the United States, it will be dominant.
For the first half-century that power was Germany: now and as far
as one can see it is the Soviet Union.

Europeans first discovered this in 1918. They discovered it
again in the Second World War. And in the reconstruction of Europe. And in the 35 years of peace that alliance with the United
States has given the continent -- by some accounts the longest
period of freedom from war since the Roman Empire. And Europe is
on the threshold of discovering it again. The Soviet Union, which
already has the power of inflicting a devastating military blow on
Europe, is moving closer to acquiring the power to inflict a devastating economic blow on it, as this can expand its influence south
toward the Persian Gulf. The direct engagement of the United
States in Southwest Asia is necessary to prevent Moscow from
gaining that power.

This underlying reality has been no less compelling for Americans. Not only would the future of an open democratic society in
America be far less promising if similar societies did not flourish
in Europe. But in an ultimate sense whoever can ally itself to
the enormous human and economic wealth of the Europeans will be
the predominant influence in the world. We realized that fleetingly
in the First World War, and then clearly after the Second World War.
We supported the Marshall Plan, NATO, European unification out of
common motive: we wanted -- and needed -- strong friends.

These, then, are the fundamental interests Europe and America
have in each other. All our compacts flow from them. Not the
other way around. Until the power of the Soviet Union finally

begins to recede -- as a result of non-Russian nationalities contesting their subjection, of economic stagnation, of changes in Eastern Europe or some development we cannot now anticipate -- these interests will not change.

2

But the balance of international relations organized around this underlying structure canted substantially in the 1970s, and is still shifting.

First, the Soviet Union has become much more powerful relative to Western Europe. The defensive aviation of the 1960s has been replaced by a rich array of attack aircraft; tank and artillery forces have been greatly expanded; naval capability in the Atlantic is expanding rapidly; and above all, well over 100 mobile medium-range nuclear missiles have been deployed, each with three warheads capable of striking any target in Europe.

Second, the United States provides less protection. Although substantial improvements have been made in the speed and scale with which the United States can reinforce NATO forces, confidence has eroded that a large-scale Soviet attack launched with little preparation could be contained. Meanwhile the deterioration of the balance in strategic weapons, as the Soviet Union has driven beyond parity and threatened to take a position of strategic advantage through much of the 1980s, has raised probing questions about the automaticity of the U.S. nuclear guarantee should war break out. And in the 1970s Europe manifestly has had much less confidence in U.S. political leadership and economic strength than it did before.

Third, for all its economic success Europe is not adding to its cohesion and power at all rapidly. The release of energy accompanying the foundation of the European Economic Community (EEC) in the 1950s and 1960s is now largely spent. In the 1970s few new common economic arrangements were added to those established earlier, while the original agricultural and budgetary institutions have become increasingly conflictive. Enlargement to the south -- to bring in Greece, Spain, and Portugal -- whatever its merits (consolidating the democratic evolution in these countries), does not marry strength to strength. Efforts to develop common European external policies have much intensified in the last years. But they are so far essentially declaratory. Germany and France added substantially to their military capability in the last decade, substantially more in relative terms than did the United States. But for Europe as a whole, real military expenditure was not much different in 1980 than in 1970.

All of these changes have occurred at a time when the prevailing doctrine of international relations -- until recently in the United States as well as in Western Europe -- has been that efforts

at detente should go hand in hand with those of defense preparedness. By "detente" most Europeans have understood the expansion
of human contact and of exchanges of goods and sustained effort at
arms control in order to relieve the tension inherent in the division of Europe. Europeans have hoped that these contacts will have
a moderating influence on the Soviet Union's behavior within and
outside its borders, but in fact if not in rhetoric these have not
made acceptable Soviet behavior a condition precedent. But detente
has brought substantial benefits to Europe and above all to Germany:
some 400,000 ethnic Germans have been repatriated from the East,
personal contacts between the two Germanies have multiplied, and
in 1979 the Common Market sold $26 billion worth of goods to the
East, including East Germany.

At the same time, the two oil shocks emphasized just how vulnerable Europe is to the loss of its Middle Eastern oil sources.
Since 1974 the European Community has made some significant progress
in reducing its dependence on imported oil. But over 60 percent
of EEC consumption is still furnished by Persian Gulf producers.

3

With trends of this kind, a major crisis was inevitable. As always
it took external shocks -- Afghanistan and the chain of events set
off by the Iranian revolution -- to reveal the situation within
the alliance.

When the Soviet Union invaded Afghanistan, the United States
reacted by curtailing or suspending its two main relationships
with the Soviet Union (agricultural trade and SALT). Europe also
condemned the invasion. Some countries, however, argued that
attempts to "punish" the U.S.S.R. would not work or advance Western
interests; they maintained trade flows and high-level meetings,
and most European countries did not join in the boycott of the
summer Olympics. The United States (and France) added substantially
to their military budgets; most other allies also made increases,
though some now have difficulties sustaining the pace.

With regard to the Middle East, the United States accepted
that the Nixon doctrine of relying on local champions was no longer
viable, and began the long, delicate, and difficult process of developing the capability to deter or combat a threat to the security of
the Persian Gulf. France and Britain quietly -- and usefully -- sent
their own naval units this fall and winter to the area off Hormuz.
But the Europeans main play was the Mideast policy launched at
Venice in June with a call for including the Palestinian Liberation
Organization in negotiations. In launching it, European leaders
argued that the problem of Palestine could not be solved without the
Palestinians. But the Venice declaration was also open to interpretation as an effort to distance Europe from the United States with
the implication that the Arabs could get a better deal from Europe.

In a word it appeared as if Europe and America had developed
different relations with the Soviet Union, and were beginning to do
so with the Middle East.

Many of my fellow diplomats have pointed out that internal crisis is the rule rather than the exception in the alliance; and that
is of course right, as far as it goes. But in 1980 the ability of
the allies to act together was only limited; harsh mutual resent-
ments surfaced; the diversity of political and military conditions
that has often been one of the assets of the alliance was widely
perceived as a liability; and thoughtful people on both sides of
the Atlantic began to ask themselves whether interests were now
diverging in a fundamental manner.

Can the situation be restored? I think it can and ultimately
will be. But it will take important internal changes -- in the
United States and in our allies -- as well as a sustained effort
to mesh differing interests through diplomacy. Meanwhile we all
will be more exposed to military pressure and political and economic
manipulation than at any time since the 1930s.

In order to succeed we shall have to get the new geometry of
world affairs right -- not just the triangle of Europe, the Soviet
Union, and the United States, but the triangle of Europe, the Middle
East, and the United States.

4

I will begin with the triangle that has the Soviet Union at its
apex.

If there is one message that comes from Europe, it is that our
friends want to see a stronger America. They recognize -- as no
doubt do the Soviets -- that it will take years to rebuild a strategic and conventional equilibrium, to relaunch U.S. economic
growth, to re-create consensus in the United States. And they
recognize that success is not guaranteed. But actions pointing in
these directions can have an enormous impact. Clearly one of the
keys to restoring the situation is U.S. domestic economic policy.

Europe must be stronger too. But I don't think that we should
have any illusions about how long it will take and how hard it
will be to re-create the economic and social conditions for a substantially greater defense effort by the allies. For Europe, 1981
will be a recession year, and even an optimistic forecast (no new
oil shock) sets EEC growth in the next five years below 3 percent
a year. Some European economists talk of an investment-led expansion developing in the early part of the decade. But there are
good supply-side reasons for being cautious about such forecasts.
In contrast to the United States, labor's share in the GNP of most
European countries jumped sharply during the first oil shock, and

has been fully rolled back only in Germany. This is a principal reason why European growth records -- other than in Germany -- were so poor in the late 1970s, and may remain poor.

But even if economic expansion in the next few years is at the high end of the scale, there are two further reasons why it will be difficult to translate overall growth into a major new military effort. One is that unemployment in the Common Market may grow from the present 7 percent to 10 percent in 1985. The other is that welfare commitments made in a time of much more bullish expectations already are difficult to sustain. Social security expenditures in the Common Market went from a fifth of GNP in 1970 to a quarter in 1979. In all but two members, the share is still rising, and in each, funding commitments under existing social legislation are the primary obstacle to even marginal increases in defense spending.

It is likely that flattening economic growth will force a cutback in social commitments, but this will take a number of years to occur. The question is whether Europe can be prosperous or secure as long as social spending continues to grow at its present rate. The United States can play a vital role in this process by its own example, and by its sustained commitment to working with the allies. But each country is going to have to find its own way around the problem.

There remains the question of the policy to be followed by the allies towards the Soviet Union.

The present official policy -- that of the "twin pillars" of defense and detente -- was adopted a decade ago. It replaced the alliance's first policy toward the U.S.S.R. -- the policy of containment, which was often interpreted as calling for the isolation of Moscow.

The premise on which detente was launched was that a stable balance of power had emerged with the accession of the Soviet Union to strategic parity with the United States. The Soviet Union was expected to be ready to become a satisfied power, more accepting of the status quo; the multiplication of personal and commercial contacts would assist the evolution.

These assumptions have not been fulfilled. Rather than slacken its effort, the Soviet Union has gone on a sustained drive for conventional and strategic primacy. Rather than becoming more accepting of the status quo, Soviet behavior has become increasingly threatening. Nor is there evidence that Moscow will permit exchanges of persons and goods, to moderate social and political conditions within the U.S.S.R. (indeed the year of Afghanistan was also the year in which the Soviets moved to snuff out remaining dissidents). Finally and most importantly, the 1980s may be the decade of new and more threatening challenges to Moscow from within its sphere of influence, if Poland is any portent.

But if the conclusions of detente policy no longer match the premises, there are few enough signs of rethinking in Europe. Detente politics has put down deep roots. Pursuit of better relations with the East is an important part of the self-image and the claim to power of many Christian and Socialist parties. Its acceptance is an integral element of many of the various left-right compromises that make European countries governable. Moreover, in a period of rising unemployment, both industry and labor argue that trade with the U.S.S.R. is, at the margin, indispensable. The mark of real commitment to a policy is when its justification is considered even more compelling when it doesn't succeed than when it does. In 1980 many European governments seemed almost desperately to be reasserting the value of detente. Only at year's end, in NATO's solemn warning on Poland in December, did new directions seem foreshadowed.

Here, it seems to me, will be one of the great opportunities for creative diplomacy in the decade. The alliance must revise its doctrine of detente, adapting it to an era in which the central dangers are that the U.S.S.R. will use its strategic advance during the 1980s in adventures outside of Europe, and in military actions against Communist states in Eastern Europe. This does not mean that either the United States or the allies should try to quarantine the U.S.S.R. and return to the Cold War. Such an effort, even if successful, would yield no more leverage than unconditional pursuit of more trade and more arms control agreements. At neither extreme does Moscow have an incentive to moderate its behavior. The real question will thus be how the allies can and should condition their ties to the U.S.S.R. on Soviet actions.

In such an approach arms control negotiations are no less important than previously. But -- and this is something that Europeans have to focus on -- when one is at a disadvantage both conventionally and strategically one must proceed even more cautiously than in an era of parity, and success will be still harder to achieve.

It is also important -- and this is something Americans should focus on -- that the United States as well as its allies conduct sustained relations with the U.S.S.R. If the United States has practically no contact with the Soviets -- as in 1980 -- other members of the alliance will find themselves tempted or thrust into the role of intermediaries, as Germany and France were last year. It is also true that if U.S. policy toward the U.S.S.R. oscillates, Europeans will take the shifts as reason why they not only can but must take matters into their own hands in developing relationships with Moscow.

No such new overall approach to Moscow can be imposed by the United States, as many Europeans thought we were attempting to do in 1980. But sustained leadership by the United States in developing and following an intellectually coherent concept is essential.

153

One of the most critical early tests of our collective ability
to deal with the Soviet Union will be execution of NATO's theatre
nuclear weapons decision. If in the next two years a number of
allies succeed in keeping their cohesion in the face of Moscow's
alternative threats and inducements, and in implementing the plan
for deployment of a new generation of cruise missiles in Europe --
or for serious, reciprocal disarmament -- we can look forward to
the future with some confidence. Either outcome would lessen two
of the most corrosive forces loose in Europe today -- Moscow's
growing ability to exercise regional nuclear blackmail, and Europe's
concern that its defense will become uncoupled from the general
defense, if the United States can only threaten general nuclear warfare in response. But governing coalitions in Germany, Belgium, and
Italy can all be subject to serious stress as this hand plays out.

Clearly the world has changed. The alliance is suffering from
an enormous lag -- trying to deal with new realities, with old doctrines, and with old hopes. The time has come -- the third since
World War II -- to attempt to reach a new consensus on how to
conduct business with Moscow.

     5

The other triangle we must get right has its apex in the Middle East.
Clearly we must be prepared for major shocks to occur there in the
1980s, as they did in the 1970s. Muslim integrism is an enormously
powerful force, and no one can now say how far it will develop.
I have three remarks to make.

First, it is important not to incorrectly specify the jeopardy.
We must not behave -- and this is a message for the Europeans --
as if the key to all Middle East politics lay in Palestine. It is
true that Palestine is one of the great human and political problems
of the area, affecting the attitudes of most Arab governments and
bearing relationship to oil supply issues. It is also true that,
unresolved, the Palestine issue can help radicalize all the Arab
regimes of the area. But it does not follow that progress on
Palestine -- however desirable -- can by itself assure the security
of Persian Gulf oil supplies. And it is worth remembering that
the balance of forces is such that a fifth Arab-Israeli war can
occur only if Egypt joins it, and only then would there be the
kind of threat of direct great-power involvement that is the ultimate danger.

It is also likely -- and this is a message Europeans often send
Americans -- that some of the most serious threats to the security
of the area will be internal and political, rather than external
and military. In such circumstances the Rapid Deployment Force might
be of little use. But the conclusion to draw is not that such a
force is not needed. It is that a competent U.S.-European Middle
East policy must prepare for a variety of contingencies -- from

Soviet intervention, to controlling the side effects of a new local war in the Persian Gulf region, to Palestine, to preventing Arab-Israeli conflict -- and not just those that fit one's favorite countermeasures. We are still a long way from that level of coherence.

Second, it is also important not to inaccurately specify remedies. If we are to engage in peacemaking -- and this is a message for the Europeans -- we should think through the implications of mediation.

The United States has been successful in successive efforts at mediation between Israel and Egypt in great part because it has been able and willing to develop relations of confidence with far-reaching political, economic, and military implications for both countries. But for a whole lot of reasons Europe's relations with Israel have withered. There is much rebuilding to do here, if Europeans want their initiative to be more than a tilt toward the oil producers.

Nor should either Americans or Europeans fool themselves that the existing oil crisis mechanism within IEA could contain a truly major shock, such as might be caused by some interruption in Saudi Arabian supplies. The existing mechanism can probably divide up available short supplies. But it cannot deal with price increases. Yet everything we know about our economies suggests that it is the price impact rather than the shortage that causes the big loss of income, jobs, and output at home. For example, CIA experts calculate that a 100 percent increase in price would after three years put output on a track 3 percent lower than it otherwise would be. The impact of such a loss on the viability of the alliance could be very great. The IEA needs to be complemented with much more powerful domestic emergency measures than now are in place.

Third, the most difficult Europe-Mideast-America issues concern who is to make what military effort where, and how to cope with the resulting increase in mutual dependence.

Development of an American force strong enough to deter -- or if necessary to combat -- an outside attempt to dominate the Persian Gulf by force would reduce the U.S. ability to meet its NATO reinforcement commitments should crises occur in Europe and Southwest Asia simultaneously. The alliance has already agreed that Europe should fill in behind the United States, providing such things as overflight facilitation, additional troop lifts, increased stocks, etc. But little has actually been done. And the required U.S. commitment could be very large.

As Europeans become more aware that such a force will in the first instance be defending interests that are more European than American -- Europe is five times as dependent on the Persian Gulf for oil as the United States -- they will wish to be consulted on decisions on how it might be used. No doubt the United States will be more responsive to such requests when they come from European countries that themselves undertake some security commitment to the area.

If you think about these three tasks -- specifying the dangers correctly, specifying the remedies correctly, dividing up the military burden -- it is already clear that an effort of cooperation and coordination will be required between us that is quite unprecedented. This brings me to the question of decision making in the alliance. Not only are the problems changing, so also are the institutions in Europe.

In 1980, for the first time on a large scale, members of the European Community coordinated their external policies. They launched their Middle East initiative, adopted a common position on Afghanistan and moved to assist Yugoslavia and Turkey, took parallel action on Iranian sanctions, and coordinated their approaches at the United Nations and at the Madrid Conference on Security and Cooperation in Europe.

These efforts are generally limited to taking common positions. The EEC has not attempted to give itself means of action (it is not a major contributor to Egypt's support, for example), nor has it been willing to try to coordinate positions when there are serious disagreements among members (as, for example, participation in the 1980 summer Olympics). Still, the frequency with which EEC foreign ministers meet and the now frequent efforts at coordination are arresting new facts in diplomacy.

I do not know how far this process will go. The Middle East initiative may be the touchstone: if it does well, yet more ambitious efforts at coordination will be undertaken.

If EEC political cooperation does take off it will shift the basis of decision making from such forums as NATO and from bilateral diplomacy -- in both of which we can play a direct role. In that case the United States and the EEC will have to find an institutional means by which they can accommodate and coordinate their positions. At present the quality of our political exchanges with the EEC as a body varies a lot, depending on who's in the chair. And occasionally we've been confronted with <u>faits</u> <u>accomplis</u>, without prior consultation.

One other possible evolution in decision making has been widely discussed -- the use of the present economic summit group (Germany, France, Britain, Italy, as well as Japan, Canada, and the United States) for political issues as well. It would have obvious advantages. But it is not clear whether such an evolution is ripe. France is still reluctant to use the summit for political considerations, and others do not want to make it into a decision-taking forum. That is (emphatically) the view of nonmembers.

Moreover, many of the most delicate decisions (for example, in regard to Middle East security issues) may be best left to normal diplomacy among the few countries that will actually be players.

The important thing to remember is that the alliance is a democracy of democracies. It can only be moved by persuasion. In the end American persuasiveness will be more important than the institutions.

7

So far I have said nothing about the management of relations within the North Atlantic area itself -- above all economic relations.

It is quite clear that we will not succeed in restoring the situation in the alliance unless we maintain an open trading system. Not only is trade the great growth industry of the West, regularly growing 1.5-2 times as fast as domestic transactions, but it is one of our most powerful anti-inflationary weapons. About one-fifth of goods output in the United States is now traded, and more than double that in the EEC.

It is also clear that there are a number of dangers ahead. The multiple reserve currency system now evolving might develop serious instability. Persistent trade imbalances could cause a relapse into protectionism. So could further, drastic increases in unemployment that now must be expected in some countries.

However, I think there are reasons to be confident that Europe and America will be able to manage pressures of these kinds should they develop. One is the strong institutions and firmly anchored habits of cooperation we have developed. Another is the success we have had this last recession year in managing the most serious trading problems -- steel, textiles, petrochemicals, autos, agriculture -- without the system snapping. And yet another is the extraordinary resiliency and adaptability of exchange and trading markets.

My guess is thus that it is likely to be the domestic economic decisions of the allies -- not their international management -- that will be the make-or-break factor.

8

In closing, let me go back to the basics.

It is true that Soviet leverage over Europe has grown. But to assert that Europe is inevitably on its way to political subjugation to Moscow -- inappropriately called "Finlandization" -- requires one to assume that Europe's leaders are fools or knaves who cannot or will not act in their own interest. They are neither. Rather, what Europeans and Americans have before them is a set of opportunities -- to begin truly to coordinate their actions in the Middle East, to adjust their policies toward the Soviet Union to new dangers, and to rethink the relationship of economic growth, welfare, and security.

One of the ironies of the alliance is that when the United States is seen as weakening in its physical strength and in its capacity to lead, it brings out not the best but the worst in Europe. If the United States provides less protection, the reaction in Europe is not to try to provide an offsetting increase in European efforts, but to balance a little more between Washington and Moscow. Something like this happened last year.

But the reverse can also be true. A strengthening United States can provide the opportunity and the incentive for a strengthening Europe. Europeans can be persuaded to do more and better if Americans do more and better.

That is why -- for all the danger of the current crisis and for all the hard effort and skill and time required to overcome it -- one can have a deep confidence in the future of the European-American relationship.

U.S. INTERESTS IN EUROPE

David Watt

The Wilson Center has posed a series of precise questions to participants in this discussion, and rather than dress up my answers in
extended essay form I intend, in order to concentrate the debate,
to answer the questions as they have been set.

I   What do you assume to be the national interests of the United
States with respect to Europe? What relative weight do you give
to security, economic, or political-ideological interests?

     I take the interests of the United States in Europe to be the
following:

     1. The preservation of free, democratic governments in West-
ern Europe willing to cooperate closely with each other and with
the United States.

     2. The preservation of prosperous European economies open to
American trade and investment and continuing to be, as they are at
present, almost an extension of the U.S. economy.

     3. The continuation of a military alliance with Western
Europe that will prevent the continent from being overrun by the
Soviet Union, and thus provide a geostrategic glacis for the United
States and also a counterweight to Soviet power worldwide.

     4. The support of European governments in

          (a) maintaining a stable world economic system and

          (b) in protecting American and European economic interests
              outside Europe.

     The first three aims, which more or less correspond to the
political-ideological, economic, and security interests mentioned

in the question, are virtually inseparable, and one cannot be given greater weight than the others. Free democratic governments can hardly be sustained on the basis of collapsing economies (as the experience of the 1920s and '30s showed) any more than they can be sustained under the threat of a vast Soviet armament without adequate military security. It is equally clear (and is becoming clearer with every threat of defense cuts) that the military alliance cannot survive without economic prosperity; nor could economic links with Europe be sustained if free governments did not survive. There is much theoretical argument possible over whether prosperity can survive the military demands now being put upon it, and another dispute is possible over whether right-wing authoritarian governments in Western Europe, such as the Greek colonels or the old Portuguese regime, could form a legitimate part of the military alliance. But to anyone taking a long-term view, these doubts are futile. The European economies need military protection, and the budgetary or inflationary strains that this protection may produce must either be borne or meliorated by successful arms control and disarmament negotiations. As for the second point, it is unthinkable that the alliance could survive the appearance of a Fascist or a Communist government in any of the main, central countries.

II   What are the most important likely developments in the region during the 1980s?

    Much depends, of course, on what happens outside the region. In particular, it is hard to make sensible forecasts without knowing (a) how Soviet policy will develop in relation to Eastern Europe, and (b) what will happen to oil prices as a result of events in the Middle East and elsewhere. In general, however, I should expect the following main lines of development.

    1. The European Economic Community   There is unlikely to be any further serious progress toward European economic integration. In fact, in some respects the situation seems doomed to slip backwards. This is not so much because of the internal contradictions of the common agricultural policy or even because of a possible British withdrawal from the European Community (with the split of the Labour Party increasingly probable this does not seem as plausible a scenario as it did six months ago). The problems arise rather from two other more fundamental difficulties. The first is the enlargement of the EEC to include Greece and probably Spain and Portugal. This is a move that has been undertaken for political reasons, but that cannot fail to complicate and sharpen the economic divisions within the EEC and loosen the whole structure. The other factor is the lamentable economic climate in general. If, as seems likely, the 1980s are a period of acute economic hardship for Western

Europe (at any rate in comparison with earlier times), economic nationalism, mercantilism, and protection are bound to increase in Europe as well as between Europe and the outside world. If overall growth is low, the differential between the inflation and productivity rates of the members of the European Community will become more pronounced, and the strains between the richer and the poorer members greater. Whether or not this leads to a two-tier European Community as some have predicted, it will certainly serve to cement still further the present close alliance of France and Germany, which seem likely to remain the most powerful and successful economies in the system, with the French economy and the franc possibly gaining ground somewhat on the German economy and the mark, though without displacing them in the lead.

While the framework of economic cooperation in Europe is going to become more rickety, on the political plane there may well be further advances. This does not mean that there is likely to be progress toward a United States of Europe of the kind envisaged by the founding fathers of the EEC. The European Parliament, for instance, is likely to find itself continuously and successfully snubbed by governments in spite of its direct election. However, external events and a shared sense of vulnerability among West Europeans may cause them to expand the political cooperation machinery that works in parallel with the EEC Council of Ministers. This will not undermine the complicated network of bilateral relationships between, say, the United States or the Soviet Union and individual European countries, but it may mean more European initiatives in relation to events in the Third World, as well as occasional united confrontations of one superpower or another. The Franco-German axis will remain the foundation of EEC developments, but we may expect to see Britain becoming increasingly implicated in and enthusiastic about them as her power continues to recede and her hankering for independent initiative abates.

2. __East-West relations__ West Europe will continue throughout the 1980s to be torn between its fear of the East and its cultural and steadily increasing economic links with the Eastern bloc. These opposing forces have produced schizophrenic symptoms in West Germany ever since the end of the Adenauer era, and the rest of the EEC countries have not been much less afflicted. We are now entering a decade in which the Soviet threat seems likely to increase, but at the same time the interpenetration of the Western and Eastern economies will also advance. The Soviet military and nuclear buildup is bound to increase fears that will be exploited for neutralist purposes by the left, but by and large Soviet actions are likely to make the task of those who urge greater military expenditure easier. The limitations on the modernization and reequipment of NATO, both at the conventional and the nuclear levels, are more likely to arise from economic than from broadly political origins. At the same time the Western need for natural gas and the Soviet need for technology are bound to increase the interdependence.

Many, perhaps most, Europeans do not see any necessary tension between these two "tracks." The one seems a natural hedge against the other. Naturally, if the Soviet Union and/or its satellites in Eastern Europe were to cut off the advantages of economic and cultural intercourse, there would be nothing West Europe could or would do to prevent it (though this is an option that is becoming more and more costly to the Soviet system). By the same token, however, there is no sign that the main Western countries intend to lower their military guard. Arms control and disarmament negotiations with the Soviet Union will be regarded, no doubt, as desirable ways of reducing expenditure and political tension, and as a means of keeping the Soviet Union "in play"; but there is no sign that the West Europeans wish to throw away any military cards for nothing or even in order to keep the Soviet Union "sweet." All the European countries seem likely to resist, to a greater or lesser extent, the proposition that the East-West situation in Europe can or should be used to regulate Soviet behavior elsewhere in the world. Clearly, if the Soviet Union were to launch a major offensive against Western interests -- say by invading Iran -- an international crisis would rapidly engulf Europe as well as the Middle East; but the European powers would show the greatest reluctance on their side to put economic links with the East at risk or to jolt the delicate fabric of political relations on the European front with the East.

3. <u>Political developments</u>   The question is whether very high levels of unemployment will swing European electorates to the left or, as has sometimes happened in the past, to the right. Since it is on the whole right-of-center governments that are presiding in Europe over the present economic crisis, some swing to the left during the 1980s out of revulsion seems probable. How far it will go, however, is hard to say. The situation is undoubtedly complicated by a number of peculiarities of personality and party structure in particular countries -- a serious, though probably not decisive swing of opinion against President Giscard appears to be taking place in France, for instance, and an important realignment of parties is appearing in Britain. More generally, the crystal ball is clouded by a cyclical revulsion against nuclear weapons and by the emergence of a number of "green" parties, which may or may not fade away. Communist Parties are not at present in particularly good shape, and while the growth of Eurocommunism, made possible by the period of detente, has been abated, presumably much to the relief of the Soviet leadership -- it seems unlikely that the Communist Parties in their harder-line guise will receive massive new support during a period of tension and Soviet military threat.

The Mediterranean members of NATO have entered the decade in better political condition than at one time seemed likely. Democracy has aparently grown enough roots in Portugal and Spain to survive various extremist threats. Italy is possibly somewhat more chaotic than it was, and Greece -- on the threshold of the Common Market -- should be able to look forward to a reasonably prosperous decade. Turkey presents a special problem, dealt with in the context of the Middle East.

III   To what extent can or should the United States seek either to accommodate to, or alternatively to modify, prevailing regional dynamics?

I do not see any serious incompatibility between the dynamics suggested in the preceding section and the objectives of American policy outlined at the beginning of my paper. This being so, the United States would be wise, in general, to let matters take their course. Pressure on Europe, as at least the last four U.S. administrations have discovered, tends to cause more trouble and tension than it resolves. The only exceptions I would make to this precept are that American governments should continue to keep up pressure on other members of NATO to maintain defense spending at a level that will keep the conventional forces of the alliance in good repair, and that they should campaign against protectionism. There is a constant tendency toward European backsliding on both, which can be overcome by constant exhortation and example. It is worth reemphasizing, however, that support across a broad political spectrum in Europe for defense expenditure depends on continuous efforts toward arms control being seen to be made.

The question of how much military contribution the European countries should make to the defense of interests outside Europe is discussed in the final section of this paper. Here I would only say that it is certainly desirable to oblige the Europeans -- both governments and public opinion -- to face their vulnerability to events and instabilities outside Europe. European parochialism is an insidious disease that needs constant attention, but that in practice yields to treatment.

Yet even if one leaves aside the parochialism issue, and the usual minor irritations such as air fares, freight rates, the extraterritorial pretensions of American law, and the host of bilateral problems that constantly arise between advanced industrial countries, it is not to be supposed that the vision of U.S. governments contenting themselves with a little discreet admonition of their allies is more than a dream. Major new sources of friction seem likely to appear on at least two fronts.

The first of these can be broadly described as the problem of the "club within a club." Ever since the foundation of the EEC in the 1950s the United States has had mixed feelings about West European unity within the alliance. On the one hand the two-pillar concept of President Kennedy has regularly been proclaimed by the United States as the model of transatlantic cooperation (not least because there is an irresistible fascination for Americans in the concept of a "United States of Europe"). On the other hand, when the EEC countries have managed to combine together effectively, as in several rounds of tariff negotiations, in the Euro-group within NATO, in the European monetary system and, more recently, in various initiatives under the political cooperation machinery, these moves have been regarded in Washington with an acute suspicion that has sometimes, but not always, been softened by time. It is, not surprisingly, hard for American administrations to grasp that European unity on almost any subject, even if it produces a position apparently hostile to immediate American interests, is usually preferable, on the long view, to chaotic bilateralism. The latest manifestation of this is the European initiative on the Arab-Israel dispute. In the American view, this is an irresponsible and self-interested meddling in a situation where the United States is the only outside participant with the ability to influence events. The Europeans reply that it is in the interest of the whole West that some part of the Western alliance should demonstrate its independence of Israeli interest narrowly defined. Similar situations may well reappear during the next decade, and all one can say about them is that (a) continuous and high-level political consultation of a kind that does not at present exist would reduce their incidence and importance and, (b) the United States should consider the possible utility in many circumstances of a "two-track" alliance approach.

The other point at which American administrations, and particularly the Reagan administration, may be tempted to twist European arms is over the future of detente in Europe. It will be apparent from what is written earlier that I am in favor, so far as possible, of keeping European detente separate from wider considerations. It is foolish to suppose that one should treat Soviet threats in widely different parts of the world in exactly the same way. Some degree of linkage, even if only atmospheric, is inevitable and, as stated earlier, at a certain level of Russian aggression it is also desirable. But detente in Europe has a life of its own that is in the Western interest to preserve, for the following reasons:

(a) Detente in Europe has in fact delivered solid advantages -- the Berlin Agreement, relative stability, greater freedom of movement across the Iron Curtain, and the (for the Russians) awkward provisions of the Helsinki Agreement, to name but a few. It is not to be lightly thrown aside.

(b) Detente has helped Eastern Europe. Granted that the Soviet Union cannot allow a complete change of regimes in Eastern Europe, and also that most Western governments fear the reunification of Germany more than they desire a massive liberalization in the Eastern bloc, an East-West balance that maintains a quiet, juridical status quo offers the best atmosphere for the gradual and limited liberalization that has been able to take place in Hungary and, until recently, in Poland.

(c) If West Germany is forced to choose between an alliance
with the United States and her continued ability to trade and traffic culturally with the East, she will choose the American alliance;
but the choice will be made under such agonizing protest that the
internal political results in the medium term would be at best unpredictable and at worst calamitous. This is emphatically a regional
dynamic to which the United States should seek accommodation.

IV   Is the pursuit of U.S. aims in the region likely (a) to complicate relationships with other regions and/or (b) to have important
U.S. domestic costs and benefits?

It may seem a mere special pleading for a European to say that
outside North America itself, Europe remains the highest American
priority in the world. Nevertheless, it can be justified in terms
of economics, of strategy, of history, but most of all in terms of
like-mindedness. The values and civilization that the United States
defends are based on European foundations, which, in spite of all the
cracks and defacement inflicted on them in the last 20 years, still
stand, and are likely to do so throughout the 1980s unless they
are overcome by military means. Without Europe the United States
would be perhaps able to survive, but she would be lonely and
frustrated to the point of madness. This priority for European
security cannot, of course, be considered as absolute. It is better
to consider the matter in terms of the degree of risk the United
States is prepared to take with its interests in one part of the
world in order to pursue them in another. Thus, to take a simple
case, if the United States were to withdraw a division from Western
Europe for the purpose of shoring up some friendly regime in the
Third World, the chances are that the American government would be
taking a risk with European security for the sake of an objective
with a much lesser degree of ultimate importance. It might still
be a reasonable thing to do, on the grounds that the risk involved
in Europe is slight and the possible gain in the Third World very
great. In other words, there are not very many direct clashes between the pursuit of American interests in one region as against the
pursuit of American interests in Europe. It is mostly a question
of nuance and shading, of a little more risk here and a little less
there.

Domestic costs are a different matter. This is largely a
question of politics. In the United States a cost that does not
have political fallout will rarely be said by most politicians, or
even bureaucrats, to be a cost at all. As determinants of policy,
it is the perceptions of disadvantage in the Congress and in public
opinion that matter more than the reality. Policies, particularly
toward Europe, may be as wise as possible, but if they can be

effectively presented as making concessions to fat cats, assisting
creeping communism, abandoning millions to Soviet tyranny, or
helping people who won't help themselves, or any of a thousand
disobliging visions of reality, they can be said to have a direct
domestic cost. They will deplete the administration's store of
political capital if proceeded with, and expose them to humiliation
and loss of credibility if not. Most of the "costs" associated
with the pursuit of American aims and interests in Europe fall
into this category.

This proposition is borne out if one looks down the list of
American policies likely to cause tensions of any kind. There are
certainly obvious tensions between, say, adequate rearmament in Europe and relations with the Soviet Union (though some of course
would say that a sound relationship is only possible on the basis
of defense parity). Equally, the cost of having greater consultation with the Europeans on strategic questions is a loss of speed
and decisiveness in the implementation of American policy. Again,
there are a few issues on which attempts to accommodate European
policies and interests outside Europe would cause genuine difficulties elsewhere. A close coordination with European governments
makes relations with the Third World and possibly with OPEC more
difficult. American acceptance of the European initiatives on
Palestine creates problems with Israel. Any tendency to improve
consultation on political and security questions causes difficulties with the Japanese, who have a legitimate voice in economic
issues but whose contribution in the security sphere does not
justify their belonging to any geostrategic inner circle.

There is another category of questions where attempts to meet
European interests must cut across real American preoccupations.
Conflict of interests over trade questions, over how to divide up
scarce oil supplies in a crisis, and over the export of nuclear
technology to Third World countries are obvious examples. The main
difficulties arise, however, where joint Western interests are
opposed by domestic problems within the United States. Arms control, joint economic and political initiatives in the Third World,
certain quarantining of East-West relations in Europe, all help to
promote American interests in Europe; but it is hardly possible to
enter into a productive transatlantic discussion of them so long
as American public opinion is in its present mood. This is a pity.

V   What should be the extra-European dimension of U.S.-European
relations in the coming period?

Since the Afghanistan crisis this question has been the most
contentious and divisive within the alliance. Now that the dust
has settled after more than a year, it seems that we have more to

agree about than we thought. It is common ground now that there is
a major threat to the crucial oil supplies of the OECD area from
political instability in the Middle East and Persian Gulf region.
This threat is made more dangerous by the demonstration in Afghanistan of a Soviet capability and willingness to intervene in the
region such as did not exist before. Exactly what forces are
appropriate to deal with these threats, or how they might be used,
is still a matter of argument among strategists and military techni-
cians. What is more important is the double agreement, first that
some Western military capability is desirable, and second that
Western Europe, whose interests are being protected alongside
those of the United States, bears some responsibility for its
creation. The question of whether this European contribution is
best made in cash, in kind, or in additional efforts in Europe
that would free American resources for concentration on the Persian
Gulf is also less important than agreement in principle that some
kind of burden sharing has to be devised. The breakthrough consists
in the realization on the part of the Europeans that they are vulnerable, that American public opinion is serious about demanding a
European contribution, and that if Europe wishes to have any influence over American policy on a matter that may mean life or death
to their economies, it had better put some stakes on the table.

So far so good. It is no longer a question of a clash of
interests, but a clash of judgments and emotions, which may be equally damaging. The question at issue -- which has, of course, its
links with the argument about detente and its "divisibility" or
otherwise -- is whether Soviet military power is the main threat
to global peace and to Western interests worldwide. It appears to
be the view of many American officials and commentators at present that it is, and that unless some new means can be found of
combating this "worldwide projection" of Soviet power, Western
positions in the Third World will become eroded and untenable, and
vital mineral and other resources will be denied to us. The European counterargument is that on the whole the Soviet menace is
vastly exaggerated; that even with the aid of surrogates such as
the Cubans it cannot be made to "stick" for very long; that the main
threat to Western energy and mineral supplies comes from regional
conflicts having little to do with the Soviets; and that an attempt
to meet extremely sensitive and complicated regional problems by
the use (or the threat of the use) of strong-arm methods would do
infinitely more harm than it would cure. A good case in point is
that of southern Africa, where most European observers believe that
the fairly relaxed, "hands-off" policy of the Carter administration
was sensible and enlightened, whereas many American critics of that
policy are now calling for tougher measures against the "Marxist"
regime of Zimbabwe and for support of counterrevolutionary forces
in Angola. Similar divergences of opinion can be found in relation
to other parts of Africa, to Latin America, and even to the Persian
Gulf region -- where European governments fear that American power
will be misapplied and will cause unnecessary disruption of oil
supplies in order to forestall nonexistent Soviet interference.

It may be said with justice that there are many parts of the
world in which Europe and the United States can agree to disagree
on such questions. Latin and Central America, certainly, are
areas where European interests are fairly tenuous today and clearly
within the ambit of the Monroe Doctrine. On the other hand, it is
possible to foresee a long vista of misunderstandings and rows on
this subject, and there is a constant danger of spillover into
more sensitive questions such as contributions in the Middle East
and detente in Europe. Some major effort has therefore to be made
to try to produce a convergence of views. The dilemma for Western
Europe is how to gain influence and standing in Washington without
actually participating in policies the European governments
consider to be dangerous if not disastrous. The problem for the
United States is to see why it should pay the faintest attention
to countries that refuse to bear any of the responsibility for
global peace. This is not perhaps the place to canvass elaborate
schemes of consultation or new institutional arrangements for the
alliance. What is clear, however, is that where the alliance is
concerned taxation and representation will have to go hand in hand
during the 1980s. If the United States desires European support
on a worldwide scale, as opposed to merely in the NATO sector, it
will have to revise its views about consultation and joint decision
making and the like. Conversely, if West Europe wishes its views
to be taken into account in Washington, it will have to take a
new look at its contribution, both in money and material, to the
preservation of peace on a worldwide scale.

DISCUSSION

U.S. NATIONAL INTERESTS IN EUROPE

A key feature of the relationship between the United States and Western Europe is the remarkable degree to which assumptions about politics and economics are shared on both sides of the Atlantic. A belief in democratic government and in a free market economy has marked the alliance from the beginning. Beyond this ideological convergence, it is the presence of the Soviet Union that has strengthened the bond between Washington and the Western European capitals. It is striking, however, that the discussion made no effort to take a fresh look at the two interrelated axioms on which U.S. policy toward Europe has rested since 1945: a) the need for a massive U.S. military presence on the European continent (at a total current yearly expense of $81 billion), and b) the assumption that the Soviet Union is ready to invade Western Europe as soon as it has an opportunity to do so. Although the introductory sections of each of the presentations provided indirect reaffirmation of these assumptions, the speakers did not question or examine them in any systematic fashion. As a result, much of the discussion was devoted to the problems and difficulties of effectively co-ordinating U.S. and Western European policies toward other areas of the world, rather than to the problem at hand, namely, U.S. interests in Europe.

What are the key challenges to be faced by the alliance in the 1980s? Thomas Enders answered directly: the Soviet military buildup and the increasing threat posed by Soviet behavior at home and abroad constitute, by far, the most serious problems. For David Watt, on the other hand, the dilemmas confronting the West have multiple roots. Contemporary international tensions grow as much from domestic political and economic problems in each of the superpowers as from the changing strategic balance.

Differences in the diagnosis of the present situation go hand in hand with important variations in policy prescriptions. Slower rates of economic growth in Europe, according to Enders, are directly caused by a larger share of national income going to social services after 1973. What is needed, then, is higher profits, lower wages, and less welfare spending. This will ensure adequate capital formation and faster-growing European economies. The United States should also take the lead in increasing its defense spending and cajoling its European allies into doing likewise. This is the only road to a strong, lean Atlantic alliance, willing and able to face the Soviet threat. Watt fully shared the opinion that Europeans will need constant prodding by Washington to keep defense spending at acceptable levels, but disagreed on the desirability of cutting social services and expenditures. One member of the audience argued that the current economic situation of high unemployment plus inflation, serious balance-of-payments difficulties, and declining older industries will not yield to simplistic treatment and that to add a drastic reduction in governmental service and welfare programs might create considerable social unrest and instability.

Several participants underlined the need to pay greater attention to Japan and its role in the Western alliance. Japan's energy needs and their impact on the Middle East situation are especially significant. The Western powers cannot include Japan only in economic summits and not consult Tokyo on global political issues. On the other hand, the Japanese themselves have been very tentative in these matters, and security leaks on their part have been a serious problem.

The Middle East is likely to continue to be the world's most explosive region, as well as one about which policy differences exist between the United States and Western Europe. Many Europeans are misled, Enders observed, in thinking that the key to all Middle East politics lies in Palestine. Others remarked, however, that the Palestinian question provides a rallying point for all of the Arab world, in a way that no other issue does, and that progress toward its solution would clear the way to other issues.

There was considerable interest in Watt's judgment that a European consensus has emerged on the need for the deployment of a sizable Western force in the Middle East (with Europe sharing part of the burden). Differences became apparent at the level of implementation. Enders stated that the purpose of the force is "...to deter -- or if necessary to combat -- an outside attempt to dominate the Persian Gulf by force." Yet, asked Watt, what happens if a breakaway government asks the Soviet Union to send in a division? Would that activate the Western RDF? And if so, for what purpose? To occupy the whole country in question or only the oil fields? And what will be done about the undoubtedly hostile indigenous population, which would have almost unlimited possibilities for sabotage? These are only some of the many quandaries confronting Western military action in the Middle East.

One participant expressed puzzlement at what she considered to be a relative lack of concern in the discussion for European involvement in Third World affairs. Recent visits by Prime Minister Seaga of Jamaica and the deputy prime minister of Singapore confirmed in her mind the need to pay greater attention to the

Third World without being defensive about Western political and
economic institutions. Others pointed out that Europeans have been
much more involved in Third World development affairs than the United
States -- in ASEAN, the Andean Pact, the Lome Agreement -- and have
sponsored much larger foreign aid programs (as percentage of GNP)
than the United States. Skepticism was also expressed at the call
for greater European military involvement in the Third World;
given U.S. experience in this regard (especially Vietnam) there is
little reason to think this would be a wise course to follow.

The Third World is clearly important to the West. But how
can the West best secure its interests, economic and political, in
the LDCs? Can the Soviet Union actually project its power to many
parts of the world in a way that can deny raw materials to the West?
Thus far, it has not. Most Third World problems, Watt asserted,
will yield to economic and political treatment rather than to
military measures. While there was agreement that Soviet leverage
over Western Europe has risen, opinion diverged on the precise
nature of that leverage. One ingredient is energy, particularly
gas. But Watt observed that energy sensitivity need not imply
that Soviet political influence is on the rise. The Western European Communist Parties are not likely to come to power in the near
future, nor has energy led, in his view, to excessively accommoda-
tionist policies toward Moscow. Enders saw, however, a gradual
tilting toward Moscow (best exemplified by Chancellor Helmut
Schmidt's visit to the Soviet Union after the Afghanistan invasion) with potentially serious implications for the future of
the alliance.

Although the absolute value of East-West trade in Europe is
high ($26 billion), in the trillion dollar economy of Western
Europe it is comparatively a small amount and should not be considered indispensable. The alliance, Enders stated, needs to develop
a new doctrine defining its objectives vis-a-vis the Soviet Union.
Containment, in the early postwar period, and subsequently detente,
performed the function well, but both have been rendered obsolete.
What is needed is a reapportionment of influence patterns in Europe.
Whereas the Soviet Union's leverage in Western Europe is on the
rise, the United States has very little influence in Eastern Europe,
and almost none in the Soviet Union. A sustained commitment to
higher defense spending by all members of the alliance could ensure
that the Soviet presence in the continent does not become over-
powering.

Watt, however, considered detente to be the best doctrine
for East-West relations. It not only has human advantages in
terms of keeping individual and family communications open; it
allows Eastern Europe to reduce its dependence on Moscow by increasing trade with the West and provides an atmosphere in which the
Soviet Union can be more relaxed about structural changes in the
Eastern European countries. It would be shortsighted of the
United States to press its allies to forego these possibilities.

REFLECTIONS

FINAL SESSION

After the six meetings organized on a regional basis, The Wilson
Center sponsored a seventh meeting designed to draw upon the earlier ones and to summarize generic themes that had emerged during
the series. We are indebted to a small "core" group of participants who attended all of the meetings and who assisted us in the
act of synthesis. We include here statements by three of the core
group members -- Robert Bowie, Roderick MacFarquhar, and Jenonne
Walker -- drawn from this concluding session. We also include
statements by two other members of the core group -- James H.
Billington and Donald Nuechterlein -- who wrote brief pieces to
provoke responses at the concluding session.

Of the notes that were struck recurrently during the series,
one was clearly domestic: a return of the U.S. economy to inno-
vative and dependable productivity is an essential precondition
to the maintenance of the open world market system that the
United States has done so much to build up since 1947. Any tendency
to adopt protectionist policies would reverberate through the
world system, with particularly disadvantageous consequences for
the newly industrializing countries of Asia and Latin America.
American confidence in the framework for world trade is necessary
if the system is to permit new entrants reasonable prospects for
development. East Asian economic policy is likely to give rise to
particularly pointed debate on these issues, not only because of
the volume of Japanese exports, but also because Korea, Hong Kong,
Taiwan, and Singapore are rapidly growing, export-oriented economies with stakes in the U.S. market.

A second recurrent note sounded in explicit or muted fashion
at every session was the necessity for thorough negotiations with
allies -- on Ostpolitik, on energy security, on deployment in the
Persian Gulf, on the sharing of defense burdens, on the recycling
of petro-dollars, on Palestinian nationalism, on southern African
and Central American policy. Although many of these issues are
embedded in a regional context that imperils policy if ignored,
each has complex connections with the policies of allies and

174

friendly nations. We can no longer assume that others will fall
into line behind our views, nor can we require that. Thus, the
reasons for varying assumptions have to be explored, differing
long-term interests of the parties acknowledged, compromises negotiated, and concerted action agreed upon. Our discussants disagreed
whether existing consultative arrangements are adequate, but all
emphasized that what matters is the will to use the institutions
we have to hammer out differences among allies and to plan outside
the context of immediate crisis.

A theme that appeared only incidentally and never became central, despite some expectations to the contrary, is the interest
of the United States in the economic development of Third World
countries. Clearly transitions from totalitarian or authoritarian
rule to more democratic governing systems and from closed, state-
controlled economies to more open ones are in the national interest
of the United States. But what means should be used to encourage
such transitions and what priority should be given to them gave
rise to controversy among our speakers, especially over Central
American and southern African issues. There was also relatively
little discussion of the degree to which U.S. support should be
conditioned upon the support of basic human rights, although
there seemed to be agreement about the legitimacy of attaching
conditions when granting foreign aid.

What follows are five different observations made during the
concluding session. These are reflective commentaries on the essays,
not systematic summaries.

Remarks by Robert Bowie

I start by noting that cooperation among allies is a topic that
was not raised by any of the initial questions. It resulted from
our discussions inescapably. I think those discussions made clear
that cooperation with allies will be crucially important during the
next decade and that it will also be extremely difficult to achieve.
Cooperation will be crucial for all the major tasks: on security,
for example, while the United States will have to take whatever
steps are necessary to restore and maintain the strategic balance,
the fact that we are living with a clear-cut parity at best will
make it essential to maintain conventional capacity, which gives
greater importance to NATO. Similarly, in the Middle East there
is going to be a need for joint efforts, not just to maintain military force, which may fall largely (but I hope not wholly) on the
United States, but to find ways of combining the political and economic relationships necessary to maintain an orderly situation
there. Economic and energy interdependence makes cooperation absolutely indispensable, to manage the supply of energy, to manage
possible interruption, to manage the economic effects of energy
price rises and of inflation, and to manage problems of monetary

transfer and their impact on the LDCs. All of these difficult
issues are going to require very active cooperation among the advanced industrial countries -- the United States, those of Western
Europe, and Japan -- and there will also have to be wider cooperation almost surely with other countries that are not thought of as
allies, but are certainly going to have to be active partners in
these efforts.

We recognize that there are serious obstacles to the kind of
concerted action that is going to be needed. The problem of cooperation has always been thorny, with lots of friction all through
the period since the Second World War, but I think it's going to
be tougher in the '80s than it has been in the previous period.
The issues themselves are more novel and more complicated than was
often true in the past. People have had little experience trying
to manage problems like those of energy and the economic strains
on domestic and international systems resulting from energy. The
Soviet Union is going to be a harder state to relate to and to
deal with in the '80s, not just because of its military power and
greater outreach, but also because I think it is going to be a
more uncertain factor with its own internal slowing economy, with
its own internal problems, with its own problems of succession.
I don't think it is going to be easy to be sure just exactly how
these will affect the way the Soviet Union looks out on the world
and what course it follows over the period of the decade. To the
extent that the Soviet Union is a more unpredictable or uncertain
factor, it will be harder for the allies to agree on how to perceive it and react to it.

The necessity of devising newer, revised stategies for NATO
in the face of parity and the need that was stressed to develop
some form of military response or capability with respect to
burden sharing in the Middle East are difficult problems on which
different countries will undoubtedly have different approaches.
They are also problems that are in the large part directly
linked to domestic politics. This linkage makes it much more
difficult for democratic states to act in concert, because the
leaders in these countries will have to use up a certain amount
of political capital that might otherwise be used for domestic
issues in order to try to achieve common approaches.

Remarks by Roderick MacFarquhar

I mentioned that policy should demonstrate both power and compassion.
By compassion I don't mean just the farsighted and to some extent
obviously self-interested generosity of the Marshall Plan and count-
less other aid efforts throughout the world, but also the reassertion
of America's traditional understanding for the process of revolution,
industrialization, and social change, which, perhaps more than any
other country in the Western world, it is equipped to understand.

We forget too often that the West, in general, and the United States, in particular, are the dynamic societies of the world, and that the Soviet Union and its allies or clients are the stagnant societies, continuing with a certain social pattern and a certain type of rule apparently without major change. A situation like Poland, where such change does appear to be taking place, illustrates this -- there immediately arises the expectation and perhaps still the prospect of a major Soviet military intervention such as has taken place in the past. So we are the dynamic societies, and the United States in particular should remember that and survey the problems it faces with that memory.

In the present American attitude toward the People's Republic of China, there is a deepening desire to understand the process of revolution, industrial development, and social change that is going on there with sympathy, and in light of a possible convergence of interest. And yet in the case of India, the power component for the United States seems so much less, and the revolution that's going on -- because it is a revolution even if it doesn't always use the language of revolution -- within a democratic framework is seen as something that is almost irrelevant, something that can be forgotten about and India itself shrugged off and allowed to become a Soviet ally. I am not suggesting that the United States should try to guide India's foreign policy. But what I am saying is that any foreign policy that combines compassion with an essential concern for power must take account of developments in countries like India, which may seem less relevant to the power balance but are of vital importance in the process of change that is going on in the world at large.

Among the more specific tasks the U.S. leadership has to address is precisely the cohesion of the alliance. While the United States has in general good relations with Japan and also good relations with Europe, the Europeans do not have such good relations with Japan. It should also be a function, it seems to me, of American leadership in cases like this to knock heads together. There is an urgent need for the European Community and Japan not to start a process of trade war that could have such debilitating consequences within the Western world. It is for the United States, which has so far I think admirably resisted the most protectionist sentiment in this country, to attempt to shape the Euro-Japanese relationship so that it is more conducive to cooperation than to confrontation. I think this involves a discussion with Japan not merely on economic affairs but also in the political arena. The Japanese are not anxious, I know, to be dragged in. That's too bad. I don't think that the United States can say, however legitimately, "It's time you picked up some of the defense tab because we have other things to do in the Middle East that are also in your behalf," without a process of bringing Japan into consultation on matters across the globe.

I want to close with the question of the importance of the
Pacific Basin, and particularly of the countries that derive their
cultural base from China. I emphasize the crucial need for the
United States to ensure that the countries in that part of the
world are brought into the world arena in the most fruitful way.
The importance of this can be illustrated by the relationship that
has developed between the United States and China. Imagine what
would be the case if China -- an enormous, powerful country, not
perhaps as powerful as its size suggests but still powerful -- had
not been brought into the world arena for the first time as a
strongly united country, in harmony with the Western world in general and with the United States in particular. Imagine the way it
was before the Sino-Soviet dispute broke out; imagine that this
vast segment of humanity, the leading figures in the greatest culture never brought under European dominance, was coming into the
world hostile to the Americans and their European and Japanese
allies. Whether the friendship between the United States and
China leads to alliance or not is for policymakers in the future,
but that the friendly relationship and the process of exploration
leading to it should continue I am absolutely certain. China is
perhaps the most important new political actor on the world stage,
and I believe that maintenance of friendship with it is absolutely
critical.

And then Japan. What Japan, and also to a lesser extent the
smaller post-Confucian countries like Singapore and Taiwan and South
Korea, exhibits is an ability to adjust to the modern industrial
world, which the United States and Europe have not yet displayed.
It has been a refrain of our meetings that the United States must
pull up its economic socks. How this is to be done has not been
made quite as clear. But I would simply point out that whereas
the Euro-American cultures and countries have provided the kind of
leadership, the kind of political setting, the kind of cultural
dynamics that have enabled industrial revolution to take place in
the West and its initial development to proceed there, it seems to
me that Japan and these other countries I mentioned, and perhaps
one day China, are adapting far more successfully to the demands
of mass industrial society. It may be that what is called for is
not budget or tax cutting, whether in Britain or America; perhaps
there are more fundamental reforms needed in our society for which
we can find cures in the Far East. The challenge that is posed
by the countries of East Asia in their different ways, China and
Japan, one political and one economic, is ultimately the most
serious challenge. If we can meet that challenge in cooperation
and friendship, then we will have an alliance that will suffer all
sorts of buffetings and setbacks, but will likely persevere. If
we fail to solve the political and economic problems inherent in
the relationships between the West and Japan and China, then I
fear that we can build up our military power as much as we like;
but the ultimate situation in the West would be far more desperate
than it seems at the moment.

Remarks by Jenonne Walker

I am skeptical of attempts to find unifying or integrating concepts among all our interests and priorities. Unfortunately, the world is not that tidy. While it seems to me inevitable that in the next few years a sense of competition with and even a fear of the Soviet Union is going to be a major preoccupation, I don't think that sense needs to conflict with other American interests in the world if we are wise about the nature of the competition with the Soviet Union and therefore about the appropriate Western responses.

I believe that the greatest area of instability and therefore of opportunity for Soviet mischief making is going to be in the Third World, and I believe that relations with our major allies, as Bob Bowie was suggesting, will be shaped very largely on how we and they see our interest in the Third World -- including how we see the nature of the Soviet threat there. An appropriate Western approach to deal with the problems in the Third World should have three broad aspects. The first is rebuilding our own economies. I think the administration realizes that this is the number one national priority. There were parts of Secretary Haig's testimony that encouraged me to believe that he realizes how important economic strength is to our foreign policy, not just because we then can afford the kind of activist foreign policy we want and need, but also because the way other countries see us -- their perception of our national will, strength, and the workability of our political system -- rests as much on our ability to control inflation and energy consumption as on the level of our defense spending. A second aspect is improving America's military forces. While one could debate endlessly exactly what kinds of improvements we need, I don't think there is any doubt that this area will get sufficient attention in the coming years.

The third aspect of a wise policy toward the Third World is not getting as much attention -- at least in public. We need a sustained effort to use America's influence and resources to try to get at some of the sources of tension and instability before they blow up and threaten our interests directly. In almost every case the only opportunity for Soviet influence in the world comes from a perception of injustice, when the sense of grievance is so great and the lack of an opportunity for peaceful redress seems so pervasive that there is resort to military conflict. The Soviets have little to offer for economic development, or as a political and social model, even for other Marxist states. Three examples from recent experience point to the importance of going to the sources of tension and instability. The successful negotiated transition to majority rule in Zimbabwe was a major success in foreclosing a potential Soviet foothold in an area of great strategic importance to the West. In the Middle East the unresolved and festering Palestinian issue seems to be a greater threat not only to Western interests in the Middle East but perhaps also to the survival of moderate regimes there than the presence of Soviet troops in Afghanistan. The third example is El Salvador. When Constantine Menges referred to the land reform program there (and I agree with him), he said that it was a major success in denying the violent left the support it needed and probably thought it was going to get from the mass of peasants. These instances suggest that doing something about the sources of tension and instability may be at least as valuable as adding a few percentage points to the defense budget.

REFLECTIONS ON THE NONMATERIAL ASPECTS OF NATIONAL INTERESTS

James H. Billington

In sophisticated circles it is sometimes hard to remember that we have nonmaterial as well as material interests. Physical security and economic well-being -- the material part of our individual and national interest -- can theoretically be defined, computed, and defended. Our relatively weakened material position in recent years has encouraged us to attempt to reassert this physical side of our national interest through demands for stronger military defense and increased economic production, if not protection. This seems an inescapable -- I would even say healthy -- response by a life-affirming entity to a deteriorating condition.

Such a reaffirmation of material self-interest is not intrinsically immoral, nor is it necessarily in conflict with the interest of others. The basic problem with the realist-materialist approach is that it is simply inadequate for expressing our own real selves.

The simple fact about Americans is that we are not just interested in guns on the border, food on the table, and toys in the playroom. What makes Americans (or any people) unique is not the material drives that we share with all people, but the nonmaterial desires that we (again, like others) feel at the deepest levels of our own culture. Since foreign policy in a democracy ultimately depends on popular consent and understanding, such policy must have secure roots at those deepest levels. Too many lives have been lost recently for ordinary people simply to leave matters to the experts. Those who would make American policy in the future must rediscover the values of the American people, if those people are to be asked -- as they surely must be in the future -- to accept hard and often uncomfortable analyses of reality.

The root values of America, which define the nonmaterial side of our national interests, may be succinctly described as God and liberty: the belief in an objective moral order within a created universe on the one hand, and in the subjective right of individual choice and fulfillment on the other. The relatively inarticulate majority of our people are surer of the first (with closely related beliefs in the family, etc.); the educated, affluent elite are surer of the second. There is a dynamic tension, if not an inherent conflict, between the two beliefs; but they have combined to create a pluralistic democracy that believes deeply in a higher authority, yet diffuses power and tolerates diversity.

In God we trust -- meaning nobody else, as Michael Novak has said. By continuing to derive their basic identity from their personal religion, Americans have resisted the temptation to make surrogate religions of impersonal political or economic theories. Democracy was rooted in a covenant before it flowered into a constitution. The sunlight of the Enlightenment did not blind our forefathers, because it came to them through a dark filter of Augustinian theology. Democracy became a theological imperative, because in Niebuhr's dictum, "Man's capacity for good makes it possible; his capacity for evil makes it indispensable."

Asking how our deepest traditions relate to others in the world today forces us to confront ideological issues and conflicts that we generally prefer to avoid in our preoccupation with short-term practicalities.

Most political power in the world today (and almost every challenge to power) is based on the authority of some revolution; and most revolutionary movements in the world today do not spring from our own tradition of revolution for political liberty, but from very different traditions that arose from the French and led to the Russian Revolution.

Our revolution essentially sought political liberty and was the climax of a series of upheavals against authoritarian monarchies by the entrepreneurial North Atlantic peoples (Dutch in the 16th century, English in the 17th, Americans in the 18th).

The French Revolution, which began as a revolution for liberty, soon gave birth to novel and rival ideals of fraternity and equality expressed in its revolutionary slogan. The causes of national and social revolution originated in these new notions of fraternite and egalite, whose goals were first expressed in two new words invented by the French in the late 1790s: nationalism and communism. Both of these ideals sought not the separation and division of power, but its concentration; not a complex constitution to defend traditional liberties within a Judeo-Christian moral framework, but new forms of centralized, secular power based on the radical simplicity of an emotional blood brotherhood or of a rationalistic egalitarian utopia.

These two revolutionary ideals have largely dominated modern global politics -- with England almost alone in upholding the tradition of economic and political liberalism until World War I, and America almost alone in picking it up after World War II.

Americans have generally understood and supported the opposition of our approximation of liberty to the Communist illusion of equality. We have not understood as fully that liberty faced a potential long-term threat from revolutionary nationalism as well as from revolutionary communism. In practice, we must worry most about the latter, but both of these ideals are inherently hostile both to our religious and to our liberal, constitutional traditions. Militant nationalism led to fascism and militant communism to Stalinism; and we face the danger of inadvertently abetting reincarnations of the former if we combat too crudely immediate threats from the latter.

The ideal of constitutional liberty has on the whole been remarkably successful in the postwar era -- far more than the Communist banner of social revolution. Not only in Germany and Japan, in Italy, Spain, and Portugal -- but also haltingly and unevenly in much of South Asia, Latin America, and Africa -- there have been advances -- contrasted to the stagnation almost everywhere in the Communist world. Except for Indochina and Cuba -- and more recently and precariously in a few other places -- there have been no clear and direct Communist gains since the immediate postwar era. With the Soviet Union facing deep internal problems and China moving away from ideological militance, the nonmaterial appeal of the Soviet example is almost entirely gone. Its assets are almost entirely material and military.

The uncommitted countries where nationalism is the dominant revolutionary passion are a testing ground for the rival claims of liberal democracy and authoritarian Leninism. Some of our greatest long-term advantages in this struggle during a time of growing political consciousness and participation are our nonmaterial ideals; but these are often either stated timidly or overlooked in our short-term preoccupation with our material interests. The very act of materially supporting resistance to a national revolutionary movement in which there is some Communist influence can associate us with so much counterrevolutionary violence as to alienate a hitherto neutral populace and heighten the chances of total Communist control.

If the liberal democratic part of our nonmaterial ideals often demands a sophisticated audience, the religious element has a far greater resonance with the masses, as evidenced by new ideological movements (in Poland, in Latin America, and perhaps even in Iran and other assertively Moslem nations): our tradition -- in direct opposition to that of the Communists -- not only tolerates but assumes belief in God among its citizenry.

A struggle seems to be coming in the uncommitted world for the soul of nationalism -- whether to link it with religious ideals and constitutional forms or with some new form of totalitarian socialism. We must not concentrate so heavily on winning short-term material battles at the price of losing the long-term spiritual war.

Our destiny as a pluralistic, yet theistic, nation may be above all to refurbish and revive our own creative example -- to show that revival of American pride does not threaten or demean others, but rather invites them in an age of increasing interchange into a broadening coalition of freedom. The discredited ideal of revolution for secular social salvation may be slowly undermined by the rediscovered reality of evolution through a constitutional system that seeks salvation in the sacred and personal realms. Standing in the monotheistic tradition of Judaism-Christianity-Islam may permit a more imaginative and hopeful reading of recent trends than the agnostic algebra of our academies presently permits us to make.

By taking seriously the nonmaterial as well as the material side of our national interest, we enter dangerous territory. There is the certainty of some hubris and hypocrisy and the possibility of new crusades or inquisitions. As we enter a period in which we shall almost certainly need to confront both Soviet and authoritarian revolutionary power with somewhat greater strength and resolve, it will be important not to create some counter-ideology of our own. We would thereby simply move back into the world of discredited political religions. Our own religions have not been political, and our politics have not been ideological.

If we can sustain, renew, and deepen our own sense of being united in plurality under a common creator, we might even begin to help point the way from a pluralistic democracy to a pluralistic world order. Different religions, colors, and political systems might learn to live and prosper together in ways that our social theorists of today can no more imagine than could the classical political theorists have imagined that democracy would be possible on a continental scale.

U.S. NATIONAL INTERESTS IN THE 1980s:
OBSERVATIONS AND CONCLUSIONS

Donald E. Nuechterlein

The six meetings held at The Wilson Center in December 1980 and
January 1981 to identify U.S. national interests in the 1980s
revealed general agreement that the United States can and should
play a large international role. Our discussions reflected none
of the self-doubt and even self-incrimination that characterized
the national debate on American foreign policy during the previous
decade. The questions raised in these meetings asked not whether,
but how the role of the United States should be played, in whose
behalf, and on the stage of which specific regions and countries.
In a world more interdependent than before, economic relationships
in particular will significantly constrain U.S. freedom of action.
American dependence on external sources of oil was viewed as only
the most visible example. Yet participants assumed that the United
States would continue to lead the Western alliance in the 1980s
and would exercise a political role in every geographical area of
the world.

Some cautioned that Washington can no longer command the NATO
allies and Japan to follow its lead on international issues.
Western Europe is now economically and politically strong enough
to resist U.S. pressure to accept its viewpoint; the major NATO
countries will insist on real consultation in all matters affecting
their interests. In the 1980s, therefore, Europe's interests may
diverge more frequently from those of the United States and Canada;
in important cases the two sides of the Atlantic may simply agree
to disagree on both their perceptions of interests and the policies
they wish to pursue.

Growing U.S. dependence on international trade and Washington's
need to accord the allies a large voice in decision making raise a
troublesome question about an assumption that was not examined in
these meetings: Does the United States really need to be heavily
involved throughout the world in order to protect its interests?
As the economic costs of a large international role grow, and as the
frustrations of leading a reluctant Western alliance system become
more apparent to Congress and the American public, this question

may become more central in American politics. We need to remind ourselves that it was only 28 years ago that the Republican Party finally accepted an internationalist rather than a nationalist foreign policy. The mood of isolationism could emerge again if the costs associated with a larger international role in the 1980s induce negative reactions among the electorate.

The Wilson Center meetings illuminated U.S. national interests in various regions of the world, but they were nevertheless limited in scope. Only in the meeting on Europe did these discussions address a number of key international issues currently troubling the United States: nuclear proliferation, international terrorism, the economic and political power of OPEC, and the threat to economic stability posed by the huge quantity of Euro-dollars floating outside the control of central banks.

To facilitate further discussion of these and other issues, I propose a conceptual framework that identifies four general categories of national interest as follows:[1]

Defense of homeland (North America) Many scholars take this narrowly defined basic interest for granted; military planners do not. Primarily concerned with the defense of the continental United States and with the strategic balance of power between the United States and the Soviet Union, this interest also includes the security of Canada's territory and air space, and the security of the Caribbean, Mexico, and the Central American states -- including Panama. As the Cuban Missile Crisis in 1962 showed, a direct Soviet threat in this area may quickly escalate to a nuclear confrontation.

Regrettably, the Wilson Center discussions completely ignored Canada and its two current internal issues: Quebec separatism and the disaffection in Western Canada over national energy policies. There was little discussion of the seriousness for U.S. internal social stability of Mexico's illegal-laborers policy. While Cuba's role in supporting Marxist factions in Nicaragua and El Salvador was discussed, we did not debate whether it would be desirable for the United States to openly confront Cuba and the Soviet Union on arms aid and guerrilla training for revolutionary groups operating in the Caribbean-Central American region.

Renewed talks with the Soviet Union on a strategic arms limitation agreement were only partially addressed in our discussions --

---

[1]See Donald E. Nuechterlein, "The Concept of National Interest: A Time For New Approaches," ORBIS, Spring 1979, for a fuller description and application of this framework.

even though it can be argued that prevention of nuclear war, and hence renewed efforts to reach a SALT III agreement with the Soviet Union, may be the single most important national interest of both countries in the 1980s.

A danger of inadequate attention to these issues is that, as security threats occur close to U.S. territory and are given wide attention by the U.S. media (El Salvador is an example), the American public and Congress may demand stronger action by policymakers to deal with these problems at the expense of broader U.S. economic and world order interests. A "Fortress North America" view of U.S. national interests could gain ground in the 1980s if there are serious political upheavals in the nearby Caribbean, Central America, Mexico, or Canada.

<u>Economic well-being (of the United States)</u>   This category includes a range of international economic issues affecting the American standard of living -- the value of the dollar, the ability of American firms to trade and invest overseas, the impact on the domestic economy of international cartels and multinational corporations, international currency transfers, and "dumping" of foreign products in the U.S. market. The Wilson Center meetings dealt with some of these issues. Participants discussed the dangers inherent in 1) OPEC's determination to raise oil prices without regard to the economic impact on the industrialized countries and on oil-poor, less-developed nations; 2) the growing U.S. dependence on foreign sources of key minerals to sustain high-technology defense and nondefense production; 3) the threat to U.S. domestic industries posed by cheaper and better-quality foreign products, produced especially in the newer industrial countries.

Despite these dangers, a large majority felt that the United States should avoid protectionism. Japan's unwillingness to limit its growing penetration of the U.S. auto market, which is causing alarm among business and labor leaders in auto-producing states where unemployment has risen sharply, came in for criticism. All participants agreed that the U.S. economy must be strengthened and U.S. productivity increased if the United States is to play a major international economic role in the 1980s.

Several speakers urged that allied countries be pressured to assume a greater share of the worldwide defense burden, because the U.S. economy may not be able to sustain simultaneously large increases in defense spending and to maintain basic domestic social welfare programs. When, and for what purposes, should the United States be willing, for example, to use its forces unilaterally if any country threatens shipping through the Strait of Hormuz? The oil shipped through that waterway is far more important to Japan and Europe than it is to the United States. Should the United

States continue to deploy major naval forces in the Mediterranean and in Northeast Asia at a time when the European and Japanese governments are fully capable economically of doing so?

Favorable world order (international security) This category encompasses most U.S. alliances, U.S. security assistance agreements with countries outside North America, regional balance-of-power considerations, Soviet support of national liberation forces, wars between non-Communist states, food shortages and world population growth, and threats to the world ecological balance. Western Europe and Japan remain vital U.S. world order interests because they contribute to international stability, and because their political and economic power is important in balancing that of the Soviet Union. But a key question is whether allied countries share the U.S. perception of international security interests and the policies required to protect them. To what extent are their national interests convergent with our own? The unwillingness of Europe, particularly West Germany, to rethink detente with Eastern Europe and the Soviet Union continues to trouble relationships with the United States. For some American leaders, this calls into question whether so much attention should be accorded to West European views in deciding U.S. policies. Similarly, Japan's reluctance to devote more of its GNP to the naval and air defense of Northeast Asia, as well as the protection of its oil life line through the Strait of Malacca, raises the question of whether the United States should defend Japan's economic interests while Japanese industrial products inundate the U.S. market. To what extent should the United States support the People's Republic of China in its economic and military goals? Is it wise to view the People's Republic of China primarily as a counterweight to the Soviet Union? Are there not dangers inherent in building up a powerful Chinese Communist state? These issues were touched upon but not fully discussed.

The growing influence of the Arab oil-producing states and the increased importance of Egypt to U.S. strategic interests in the Middle East forcefully raise questions about the validity of Israel's intransigent policy on the Palestinian homeland issue and of its illegal annexation of East Jerusalem. As the American public becomes more aware of the trade-offs in the Middle East, it may insist upon a broader view of Middle Eastern issues than past Israeli policy has permitted.

Promotion of values (ideology) Our discussions indicated general support for continued emphasis on human rights in American foreign policy. In Africa, the United States should continue to press the government of South Africa to alter its repressive racial policies; in Latin America, U.S. policy should continue to encourage existing military regimes to hold elections and to permit democratic opposition groups to function. The United States should press those allies with highly authoritarian governments (South Korea and the Philippines, for example) to liberalize their rule, certainly to the extent that citizens are not imprisoned solely for holding views contrary to official policy.

However, there was also support for the view that U.S. policy should not try to promote Western-type democratic systems in Asia and African countries where there is neither an historical nor an economic basis for assuming that such a government could effectively function. Latin America has a different tradition, and here the liberalization process ought to be pressed by U.S. policymakers. Yet this effort should be made quietly and without engendering the deep resentment against the United States that has occurred in Argentina and Brazil during recent years.

With regard to the Soviet Union and other Communist countries, the United States should insist on implementation of the pledges made in the Helsinki Agreements to permit greater freedom for citizens in their societies. The United States should not be less vigorous in pressing its ideas of liberty on left totalitarian regimes than it is on rightist authoritarian ones.

Conclusion   Although the Wilson Center meetings gave greatest attention, and presumably the highest priority, to world order and international economic interests, this judgment may not correspond with political realities within this country during the 1980s. The holding of American diplomats hostage in Iran and Colombia, the growing evidence of Soviet and Cuban involvement in revolutions in Central America, and the social dislocations caused by the large influx of Latin American refugees to the United States during the past year point up for me the inability of Washington to deal effectively with threats to U.S. citizens, U.S. borders, and U.S. interests in the Caribbean area. Coupled with this is our inability to formulate a viable policy regarding 5-7 million illegal laborers from Mexico who put demands on U.S. social services and educational facilities. The huge increase in narcotics traffic into the United States from Central and South America is another example of a threat to American society -- from an area proximate to U.S. borders, not from far-off Laos or Burma. As these problems multiply and capture public attention, Washington will be obliged to give them greater heed -- sometimes at the expense of world order and economic interests elsewhere in the world.

In 1968, the Congress established The Woodrow Wilson
International Center for Scholars as an international
institute for advanced study and the nation's official
"living memorial" to the 28th president, "symbolizing
and strengthening the fruitful relation between the
world of learning and the word of public affairs."

The Center opened in October 1970 and was placed in
the Smithsonian Institution under its own
presidentially appointed board of trustees.
Its chairmen of the board have been Hubert H.
Humphrey, William J. Baroody, Sr., and, currently,
Max M. Kampelman.

Open annual competitions have brought more than
350 fellows to the Center since 1970. All fellows
carry out advanced research, write books, and join in
seminars and dialogues with other scholars, public
officials, members of Congress, newsmen, business
and labor leaders. The Center is housed in the original
Smithsonian "castle" on the Mall in the nation's
capital. Financing comes from both private sources
and an annual congressional appropriation. The
Center seeks diversity of scholarly enterprise
and of points of view.

ISBN (Perfect): 0-8191-1787-0